THE OBJECTIVE PATH

FOR US EVERYDAY PEOPLE

DAN HOEGER

TATE PUBLISHING, LLC

Nihil Obstat:
  Rev. Richard L. Schaefer
  Censor Deputatus

Imprimatur:
  Most Rev. Jerome Hanus, O.S.B
  Archbishop of Dubuque

About the Author

Dan Hoeger was ordained as clergy of the Roman Catholic Church as a Permanent Deacon in September 1989. Following ordination, he remained in private business and also served as a professional volunteer minister of the Church. In January of 2002, after a successful business career of 30 years,  he retired from business and subsequently entered full time church ministry by joining the staff of St. Patrick Catholic Church in Cedar Rapids, Iowa—a parish with a current membership of approximately 3,000 individuals.

In addition to his parish responsibilities, Deacon Dan also serves on a number of boards and commissions for the Archdiocese of Dubuque, is very active as a Chaplain for the Cedar Rapids Police Department, and serves as a member of the Criminal & Juvenile Justice Commission for the State of Iowa.

He and his wife Rosemary have been married for 36 years and have six adult children and seven grandchildren.

A few years back, *The Cedar Rapids Gazette* ran a ¼ page feature article on Deacon Dan entitled,

"A Capitalist and a Chaplain." It is from that viewpoint, plus that of a family man, that he brings his experiences, training, and wisdom to *The Objective Path for Us Everyday People.*

Dan is available for public speaking engagements for Key Note Address on topics as covered in this book. He is also available as a retreat director for both religious and business retreats. For information on available dates and topics, he can be reached via e-mail at deacondancr@aol.com or through his publisher.

Dedication

I dedicate this book to my parents, Tony and Gladys Hoeger. I am convinced that without the firm foundation of the solid faith they had instilled in me as part of my total upbringing, that my life, my accomplishments, and my ability to tackle the problems of everyday life would have been drastically different. I pray that with God's grace and guidance I can pass that same faith, which I have been so blessed with, on to my own children and grandchildren.

I'd also like to dedicate this book to my wife Rosie, the love of my life for the past 37 years. As partners in life, we have traveled together down a road, that while for sure not always paved with gold bricks and lined with sweet smelling roses, yet by the faith we have shared, we've been able to climb the sometimes steep hills and maneuver around what at the time appeared to be the most difficult of obstacles.

Table of Contents

Introduction

We have created for ourselves a world that is running at such a fast pace, that for most of us, we are finding it more and more difficult just to keep up. Our lives and the schedules we keep are filled daily with places to be, people to meet, obligations to fulfill, and fires to put out. Furthermore, it is at a pace that has become almost unmanageable. Families are finding themselves coming and going at such a hectic pace that on many days, they are lucky to meet each other for a few brief moments in passing. Our calendars and our schedules are so packed with activities that most families could use the assistance of a professional social secretary just to make sure that everyone is where they need to be, on what day, and at what time.

Additionally, our levels of stress and anxiety have increased to the point where it is no longer just an occasional occurrence; rather, for most of us it is almost a way of life.

Yet we want to live the American dream. And for most of us, that American dream is to have it all. We want everything that this land of opportunity has to offer. We want all the material things that we think will make us happy; we want all the money that we think will give us security; we want the positions in our work and our social lives that we think will make us feel valued; and we want the relationships that we think will make us feel loved.

But is that possible? Is it possible to even think that we can have it all? Is it possible to think that we can have it all, and still *have a life*? And most importantly, is it possible to think we can have it all and still live a life as a good Christian?

The purpose of this book is to provide a little additional insight into those questions. It is the intent of this book to help bring a little sense of order, meaning, value, reason, love, and yes, even a little fun and pleasure into your life. Not only to live that life in the world as it exists today, but more importantly, to live it as a good Christian in the manner and according to teachings of our Creator and God. The purpose of this book is to help you have a life and live it to the fullest.

Any carpenter or woodworker will tell you that when one works with wood, it is always better to work with the grain than against it. The purpose of this book is to help you work "with the grain" of the world and the society we live in, not against it, while still living the life of a good Christian according to the teaching of Scripture.

Woodrow Wilson once said, "The man who is swimming against the stream knows the strength of it." Most of us are well aware of the strength of the stream we are up against with the rat race of the world and the values of the society we live in. Rather than constantly fighting the strength of the steam, it sometimes makes more sense to let the stream go around you rather than constantly fighting its strength by going against it. *But*, as you are floating with the strength and current of the stream, make sure you are at least in a good strong canoe with a good paddle, for at least then *you* will have control over where you will end up. This book will help provide you with the canoe and the paddle. The purpose of this book is to help give you control of your life, rather than allowing the events of life to control you.

chapter one

The Starting Point

For about 30 years of my adult life I was a part of the business world. In that world, I assumed that God had put me on this earth to be successful. It was my assumption that if I did not use the time, talents, and energies he gave me to achieve that success (*the success that I wanted*) then I was not fulfilling the purpose for which he created me. Thus I would be missing my call.

One of the lessons I learned early on in my business career was that working hard was only one part of the equation to success. The other and probably the most important, is that I also needed to work smart. While there are many ingredients that go into a person's ability to working smart, one that I learned early on was that it was absolutely necessary to adopt the strict practice of establishing goals. So from the very beginning of my career, I attended virtually every seminar available on the topic so that I could learn the best and most effective ways of establishing the goals I needed to assure my success. I read book after book on the topic, and soon learned the difference between a simple wish and a solid goal. There is a Japanese Proverb that says, "Life without a goal is like entering a jewel mine and coming out with empty hands." I didn't want to come out of the jewel mine with empty hands; I wanted all that this land of opportunity had to offer.

Almost without exception, every seminar and every book stressed that a life without a clear set of goals that identified and described one's desired destination is like a ship wandering aimlessly in the wide-open sea. Like a ship that is sailing the wide-open sea and on the move constantly day in and day out, so to with our lives; even if we are on a constant move but do not have a clear goal for our desired destination, once we do enter a port-of-call, we will never know if we are where we should be, or if the port we are in is where we wanted or hoped to be. Of course, the worst situation is when we wander aimlessly through life and we never arrived at *any* port-of-call.

So I was convinced, brainwashed, indoctrinated - use whatever words you wish - but for me the importance of setting goals became very much a part of my life. I discovered that the more effort and seriousness I put into the establishing of my goals, the more I succeeded in my goals becoming a reality. The more success I enjoyed, the more convinced I became of the value of establishing goals. Napoleon Hill stated it very clearly when he wrote, "Reduce your plan to writing. The moment you complete this, you will have definitely given concrete form to the intangible desire."

Establishing goals became important not only

to me on a personal level, but because I felt so strong about it and was so convinced of its value, I also introduced goal-setting as a regular and routine practice for my entire staff. At the beginning of each calendar year, I strongly encouraged everyone to complete a goal-setting exercise for themselves. It was always my firm conviction that a sure way to assist in the company's success would be for each member of my staff to also experience their own personal success. And for them to succeed, I felt it was necessary that they also establish their own goals. I was convinced that without a clear set of written goals, one would not have a meaningful yardstick to effectively measure success, or their lack of it. As Henry Kissinger put it, "If you don't know where you are going, every road will get you nowhere." I wanted my staff to know not only where they were going, but I also wanted them to know when they got there. Before they could set their goals and reach out for the next higher plateau, they first needed to be able to identify each of their plateaus of success along the way.

So each year we religiously held goal-setting sessions with the entire staff. And each year, I could clearly identify those employees who took their goals setting exercise seriously from those who considered it just another item on the company agenda that we do every year. Over the years, the more I observed employees, the more I discovered that those who were serious about their goals had several things in common.

1. They were generally the employees who were the happiest with their jobs.

2. They displayed more of a confidence in their positions.

3. They appeared to have their jobs more under control.

4. They were better able to cope with problems, challenges, and disappointments inherent to any position.

5. They were the employees who worked better as a member of the team.

6. They displayed less frustration, and were less irritable when the day was not going entirely their way.

7. They had less absenteeism and fewer sick days.

8. They were more productive.

Bottom line, as a general rule, I found them to be the most successful and the most valuable employees to the company.

But why was that true? What is it about setting a few goals that could possibly provide that many positive results? How could the simple setting of goals help with employee absenteeism or fewer days off for illness? Why would an employee be able to better cope with problems, challenges, or disappointments simply due to their writing a few goals on a piece of paper?

Well, if the setting of one's goals were simply a matter of putting a few items that we would like to have on a piece of paper much like that of writing a letter to Santa, then the questions would be valid. One would have every right to question the validity and value of establishing goals. There would be very little benefit in even taking the time for the exercise. But establishing goals is a very serious business. It takes a lot of sincere thought and time to properly establish goals. And then, once they are established, they cannot be simply put away in a drawer, filed safely away till next year, only to be reopened like a time capsule to see how we did.

But this book is not about how to, or even the benefits of establishing good business goals. It's not about how to get rich. It's not about how to successfully move up the corporate ladder in the shortest possible time. It's not about how to do more, or get more accomplished in a 40 to 60 hour work week. If that is what you are looking for, you can put this book down now and return to the bookstore, as there are all sorts of other excellent books available on the market on those topics. This book, however, is not one of them.

This book is about your life and how to live it to the fullest. But before we can live our lives to the fullest, and before we can have whatever our definition of *"it all"* is, we must first have and maintain full control over our lives. For all too many of us today, life is totally out of control. It has been said many times that if you don't run your life, somebody else will. The key is for you to run your life, not others or especially outside circumstances.

Through the forthcoming chapters of this book, we are going to examine various ideas that will assist you in putting together your *Life's Strategic Plan.* We will discuss proven methods for taking control of your life so that *"you"* can run your life, rather than simply allowing the events of your life to run you. This book will help to give you control of your life, rather than the events or circumstances of your life having control of you.

Any successful business manager will attest that for a business to be managed successfully, the most elementary rule is to *"Manage by Objective."* When we don't, can't, or forget to manage the business by its objective, we then slip into, or are forced into "management by crises." Unfortunately for most of us today, life is being managed far more by *"crises"* than by *"objective."* For too many people today, life is running them, rather then them running their life. Life is happening to them, but they're not having a life. In our world today, few families are working toward the same objective. Living is one thing; having a life is something different, and they are often far from being the same.

It's time that we start to take control over our

lives. It's time that we quit managing so much of our lives by living from one crisis to another. It's time to give very serious thought and deliberation to what the objective of life is, and then put together our *Life's Strategic Plan*, for then and only then can we begin to manage our lives by our true objective. Then and only then can we live our lives in the way that our Creator and God intends for our life to be here on earth.

To do that, however, takes some serious thought; it takes time; it takes work. It will take *you* to do it. As Thomas Edison said, "I never did any- thing worth doing by accident, nor did any of my inventions come by accident . . . they came by work." In the same way, life takes work. Once in a while the desperation pass will be successful, but we cannot win the game counting on that type of play.

So then, let's go to work. Let's get serious, roll up our sleeves, and put together our *Life's Stra- tegic Plan*. But I caution you, remember the words of Ralph Waldo Emerson when he said, "Beware of what you set your heart upon, for it shall surely be yours."

The True Wealth

Happy the man who finds wisdom,
the man who gains understanding!
For her profit is better than profit in silver,
and better than gold is her revenue;
She is more precious than corals,
and none of your choice possessions can compare with her.
Long life is in her right hand, in
her lift are riches and honor;
Her ways are pleasant ways, and
all her paths are peace;
She is a tree of life to those who grasp her,
and he is happy who holds her fast.

(Proverbs 3:13–18)

chapter two

The Reason for the Objective

As discussed in the previous chapter, any businessperson will confirm that in order to be successful in the managing of *any* business, one needs to "manage by objective." To do that, first you need not only to have a very basic and clear understanding of what the business is all about, but you also need a comprehensive understanding of why the business exists in the first place. If we are ignorant on these very basic facts, we can never hope to accomplish the objective of the business. If we do not know the "objective" of the business, it will be near impossible to effectively, much less successfully, "manage" the business.

The same is true with life. Most people go through life without giving much thought to how they can better manage their life, much less ever giving consideration as to what the objective of life is really all about. It's no surprise then that for so many, life is running totally out of control.

Failure to have a good understanding of the true objective of life causes several problems:

- We tend to define our lives more on what we *"do"* rather than on who we *"are."*

- We tend to consider life as being a success or failure almost entirely on the degree of success or failure we experience in what we *"do"* in life.

- When we equate our success so closely to what we *"do,"* we also tend to relate happiness to the success we have in our *"doing."* And when that is the case, we tend to place the majority of life's emphasis on the necessity for *"doing"* more.

- Because we have more of a focus on the *"doing"* rather than the *"being,"* life becomes a matter of *"doing something"* rather than *"being someone."*

- And when our focus is on the *"doing"* rather than on the *"being,"* we tend to have our lives ruled by *"what"* we need to do, rather than by the *"why"* we do things in the first place.

It has been said that in our fast-paced society today, we have become much better at living as *"human-doings"* than we are at living as *"human-beings."* That is not what our God had intended the

"Objective" of our lives to be.

Because we are much more concerned with our success in "*doing*" rather than our success in "*being*," our definition of happiness is being skewed and distorted to the point that not only are we are suffering, but our marriages, our families, our churches, and our communities are also suffering.

Happiness resulting from the success we achieve strictly and only from the "*doing*" is usually short-term in nature, compared to the happiness resulting from the success we achieve as a result of our "*being*."

Unfortunately, because our definition of happiness is being skewed and distorted for the sake of getting things done, people today tend to be much more concerned with the short-term happiness that comes from the success in "*doing*" than they are on long-term happiness that comes from the success in "*being*."

Perhaps you doubt this. After all, isn't happiness really what we hope to attain from the success of our endeavors? Isn't that why we are working from sun up to sun down? Isn't the reason that we are living the lifestyle that we are, because we believe our chosen path in life is our pursuit to happiness? One would sure think so, wouldn't you? But so often, this is not the case.

It's when we fail to have a focus on life's "Objective" that we tend to focus more on what's going to make us happy only for *today*.

It's when we fail to have a focus on life's

"Objective" that we become more focused on just getting through to the end of the month, rather than being focused on life and on the true "Objective" of life.

It's when we fail to have a focus on life's true "Objective" that we often find ourselves jumping from one thing to "do" to another. Our lives become cluttered, hurried, mismanaged, and out of control. It's at times like this that, as the old saying that goes, *"the hurryer I go, the behinder I get"* really becomes a reality in our lives. All to many times, our lives become so cluttered and busy with activities that we tend to confuse our activities with a since of accomplishment. When that happens, too many times we are finding ourselves in a situation of only spinning our wheels at 90 miles per hour, but yet going nowhere.

By going through life in such a manner, while we may ultimately find ourselves, so to speak, in a "port-of-call," we may discover that where we ended up may not really be where we wanted to go in the first place.

It's been said that when you die, you will be shown as a birth date, a death date, and a dash between. We want to live our lives so that people will remember the dash, not the numbers. The dash will not be just the "doing" in life, but above all, the "living."

In Scripture we read, "But when I turned to all the works that my hands had wrought, and to the toil at which I had taken such pains, behold! All was vanity and a chase after the wind, with nothing gained under the sun." (Ecclesiastes. 2:11)

Life does not have to be a matter of chasing the wind. We are reminded in the above Scripture that while we can have our schedules filled with things to do and places to be, we naturally feel that we should be accomplishing something. Yet at the end of the day, we may find nothing but exhaustion and frustration. As the actress Lily Tomlin once said, "The trouble with a rat race is that even if you win, you're still a rat." How often, at the end of our day, do we not feel like rats in a maze?

The answer is in the wisdom of the "Objective" of life, not in life's chaotic schedule.

Planning Pays

My son, let not these slip out of your sight;
Keep advice and counsel in view,
So will they be life to your soul, and
an adornment for your neck.
Then you may securely go your way;
Your foot will never stumble;
When you lie down, you need not be afraid,
when you rest, your sleep will be sweet.

(Proverbs 3:21–24)

chapter three

Determining
the Objective

If you were asked the question, "What is the objective of your life?" what would your answer be? Before you read any further, I would ask that you ponder that question and arrive at an answer.

Okay, do you have your answer in your mind? If not give it some more thought. We are not in a hurry, after all we are working on your *Life's Strategic Plan,* so take your time. Your *Life's Strategic Plan* indeed does merit a few extra minutes to giving this question some very serious thought. *"What is the objective of your life?"*

Now that you have arrived at your answer, I would again remind you of the question I had asked: *"What is the objective of your life?"* Note that I did not ask, *"What is your objective in life?"* And there is a definite difference between the two questions.

The question: *"What IS the objective OF your life?"* implies that there is already an objective in place. On the other hand, the second question puts the emphases on the word "your." The question *"What is YOUR objective in life?"* implies that life's objective is in your hands to establish.

The first question is a *"Why am I here?"* question, whereas the second is more of a *"What am I going to do here?"* question.

I make a point to distinguish the difference between the two because it has a direct bearing on our understanding of the "Objective" of your life. For most of us, we approach our objective as something that we can establish or have a direct control over. Maybe we answered the question by saying something like, "My objective in life is to be a success in my career" or "My objective in life is to become financially independent" or "my objective in life is to be happy," or "my objective in life is to a good parent, (or a good spouse, or good employer, or a good citizen)." While all these answers may be worthy goals in life, they are not the "Objective" of your life.

The "Objective" of your life, as I am defining it here, is a *"Why am I alive on this earth?"* type of statement. Why did God create me? What is the reason for my existence? What is the purpose and reason God has for putting me on this earth at the time in history, and in the family and society that he did? Why did he give me the talents and gifts that he did?

To understand the "Objective" of life, we need to start from where it all began. We need to start with our Creator. Only by starting with him and the revelation he has given to us can we discover the point, the purpose, the meaning, and the "Objective" of our lives.

Remember back to the analogy of managing a business by its objective? In order to do that, we need to go back to when the business was founded, when it was created, and we need to look to the one who first conceived the thought and reason for creating the company. We need to discover the "*Why*" the company exists. Once we learn that, we can then know the objective.

As stated earlier, to manage our lives successfully we also need to first understand the "Objective" of our lives. And to get those answers we need to go to the one who conceived the thought to create us in the first place. That, naturally, is our Creator, our God and Savior. For without understanding and recognizing our God's objective for life, at the very best, all our efforts, hard work, sweat, tears and toil in this life would only be temporary. Without understanding and recognizing our God's objective for life, regardless of any temporary success we may experience, life would be virtually meaningless - here today and gone tomorrow. Without understanding and recognizing God's objective for life, our lives can run out of control, many times without making any sense.

On the other hand, when our God's objective" is the footing and foundation of our lives, life takes on an entire new meaning and purpose. When our God's objective is the footing and foundation of our lives, and when at those times life forces us to change our plans along the way, we can look at it as simply that: a change in plans - nothing more, nothing less - for our objective remains the same.

But before we get into what his objective for

life may be, it's necessary that we first take a closer look at the author of the "Objective," for we will give no more value to the "Objective" than we do to the author.

In Psalm 100:3a we read, "Know that the Lord is God, he made us, his we are." Survey after survey indicates that the majority of Americans do, in fact, believe in God. According to what we are telling the pollsters, the vast majority of us state that we do acknowledge that there is a God who is the Creator of all. However, a number of recent surveys conducted by The Gallop Organization reveals some very interesting information.

In May of 2004, their surveys found that 81% of Americans say they believe in heaven, 10% say they are unsure, and only 8% state they do not believe.[1] These statistics aren't bad. However, while 81% state that they believe in heaven, an article published on March 23, 2004, and written by Frank Newport, Editor in Chief of The Gallup Organization, informs us based on surveys taken in 2003 that only about 66% of American adults report being a member of a specific church or synagogue, and only 61% of those surveyed stated that religion was important in their own lives.[2]

Then in early June of 2004, another survey reported that only 43% of those surveyed indicated they had attended their church or synagogue services in the past week.[3]

Additionally, in a poll conducted as recently as January 2005, only 55% of Americans felt that they were at least somewhat satisfied with the amount of influence religion was having on our society today. [4]

Think about those statistics for a moment. Out of every 100 Americans adults, 81% profess to believe in a heaven and a life hereafter, and yet only about 67% belong to a church or synagogue. Even of those who state they belong to a church or synagogue, only 61% feel that religion is important in their lives. And even of those, only 43% attended their church or synagogue in the past week. Based on those statistics, it is no wonder polls indicate that only 55% of us are satisfied with the amount of influence religion is having on our society today. The reality is that religion cannot and will not have any more of an influence in our society than it has in our lives as individuals.

We have been indoctrinated for so long with slogans and attitudes like that of "separation of church and state" and "religion is a private matter" and warnings to "stay away from two topics of conversation; religion and politics" and countless other slogans and attitudes, that true apathy has become the norm with our faith life and our relationship with our Creator and God.

I would like to share with you a little story that I think epitomizes where all too many of us are at with our faith and the relationship we have with our God. It goes like this:

Once upon a time, not all too long ago,
Satan was training a new class of recruits,

and as part of their training he gave to each of them the following assignment. He told them that each was to arrive at an idea that would lead more of the human race away from their God and bring them to him in hell. After several days of contemplating and working on the assignment, it came time for the new recruits to present their idea to their boss.

The first recruit said his idea was to bring about a terrible natural disaster upon the whole earth, one so bad that it would cause wide spread disease, hunger, and total chaos among the people. "Surely," he said, "they would blame God for this and turn away from him."

"No," Satan said, "I have done that many times before in history, and each time the opposite happens, they only run to God all the more."

The second recruit then presented his idea. He said that he would cause the people to begin fighting with each other. He would create an atmosphere where the whole world would be at war, causing bloodshed such has never been seen in the history of man. "Surely," he said, "with this hatred and bloodshed upon the earth, they would blame God and turn away from him."

Again Satan said, "No, I tried that many times also, it didn't help. The more bloodshed there is, the more they look to their God for guidance, comfort, support, and wisdom."

Finally the third recruit presented his idea. He proposed they create a society that has everything. Give them all sorts of comforts in their lives. Give them a good economy. Give them knowledge and information like they could never imagine. Give them the ability to cure most any disease that may come upon them. Give them the ability to fly to the moon if they wish. And then they'd instill into the hearts of the humans an attitude of apathy toward their God. His proposal dictated they wouldn't have do anything to try to turn the people away from God, all they'd do is give them enough good things and they will develop an attitude of indifference toward him. With enough pleasures in their lives and a little apathy in their heart, they will begin to feel that they don't really need him. They wouldn't have to "turn" the humans away from God, for they will simply "fall" away by themselves. How much easier could it be?

I wonder sometimes if that is where we are at today. Has Satan become successful with his plan of instilling apathy toward our God into our hearts? Has life become so good with all our luxuries, all our education, and all the information and technology at our disposal, that we no longer feel a need for God? We don't deny his existence in the least. Overwhelmingly, we say we believe in him and life after death. We are not mad at him, but yet, have we become indifferent to him? If that's not the case, why is it, then, that far less than half of us who say we believe actually attend our churches and worship our God on regular and routine bases?

We can give no validity to the "Objective" of life until we first give full and undisputable validity to its author. So before we talk more about the "Objective," let's first spend a few minutes getting a better understanding of the author, the originator of the "Objective" of our lives. It's not just another important step in putting together your *Life's Strategic Plan*. It is the *most important* step.

Praise to You O Lord on High

Give to the Lord the glory due his name;
adore the Lord in holy attire.
The voice of the Lord is over the waters,
the God of glory thunders,
the Lord over vast waters.
The voice of the Lord is mighty;
the voice of the Lord is majestic.
The Lord is enthroned as king forever.
May the Lord give strength to his people.

(Psalm 29:2–4, 10b-11)

chapter four

The Author

Having only an inborn knowledge of God is just the beginning. Having a belief in God, and believing God, is not the same thing. Knowing of God, and knowing God, is also something different.

The statement, *"God is God, Because God is God"* is so simple, yet so powerful and so packed with meaning. Think for a minute of the majestic nature of our God. A God who is all-knowing and all-powerful. A God who always was and always will be. A God who is the creator of everything. As it states in Scripture, "For from him and through him and for him all things are." (Romans 11:36a)

Think of the last time that you lay out under the stars on a warm summer night and marveled at the universe that holds them.

Think of the last time you flew in an airplane and had a different perspective on the beauty and the makeup of this land in which we live. And if you have ever ridden in an airplane at night, recall how as your plane approached one of our larger metropolitan cities, and as you quietly stared out the window, you noticed all the lights and all the cars so busy in their coming and going. You noticed all the buildings and quietly wondered what they were all used for and pondered how all those buildings played such an important role in the lives of so many. And then to think how loving our God must be to desire a personal relationship, and to be involved in the lives of each and every one of so many individuals below.

Or think of the last time you saw pictures of outer space and realized just how small the world we live in really is compared to the limitlessness of space and everything in it.

Even with all that taken into consideration, we still cannot even begin to come close to comprehending the majestic magnitude of our God. It's almost beyond belief that anyone could possibly have the slightest degree of apathy toward such a great and wondrous and loving God as we have.

Many times in Sacred Scripture we are given examples of God's majesty and power. One such example is when God responded to Job after he questioned the wisdom of the Lord. Listen to how the Lord responded to Job:

> Then the Lord addressed Job out of the storm and said: Who is this that obscures divine plans with words of ignorance? Gird up your loins now, like a man; I will question you, and you tell me the answer.
>
> Where were you when I founded the earth? Tell me if you have understanding. Who determined its size; do you know? Who stretched out the measuring line for it? Into what were its pedestals sunk, and

who laid the cornerstone, while the morning stars sang in chorus and all the sons of God shouted for joy?

And who shut within doors the sea, when it burst forth from the womb; when I made the clouds its garment and thick darkness its swaddling bands? When I set limits for it and fastened the bar of its door, and said: Thus far shall you come but no farther, and here shall your proud waves be stilled!

Have you ever in your lifetime commanded the morning and shown the dawn its place, for taking hold of the ends of the earth till the wicked are shaken from its surface? The earth is changed as is clay by the seal, and dried as though it were a garment.

Have you entered into the sources of the sea, or walked about in the depth of the abyss? Have the gates of death been shown to you, or have you seen the gates of darkness? Have you comprehended the breadth of the earth?

Tell me if you know all: Which is the way to the dwelling place of light, and where is the abode of darkness, that you may take them to their boundaries and set them on their homeward paths? You know, because you were born before them, and the number of your years is great! (Job 38:1–14; 16–21)

Of course God was being facetious with Job as he finishes his questioning. Job was at the point in his life that he was questioning the validity of God's wisdom. God's questioning made Job face the reality of God. The questions helped Job come to the realization that "*God is God, Because God is God.*" And it is toward that one and only and same God that we have the arrogance to develop a sense of apathy.

In the first chapter of the letter of Paul to the Colossians we hear, "In him *everything* in heaven and on earth was created, things visible and invisible . . . *all things* were created through him, and for him. He is before all else that is. In him *everything* continues in being." [emphasis added] (Col. 1:16–17) Everything then, absolutely everything came from him. He is the God of the universe. This is the God of all creation, the God to whom we owe our very existence.

There is this little story about this highly intelligent scientist who was having a debate with God on the creation of the human race. The scientist, ever so clever, said to God, "Well, the making of a human is not all that difficult, as we have now discovered the DNA make-up of a human. We have come to understand the cells of the body and the placement of each. We have discovered how to clone and we, too, can create a human being."

And God said, "Yes my son, I have given you the mental capacity and even the tools to discover what goes into the biological make-up of my most precious and cherished creation, but," He said, "when

I first created man, out of love I formed him from the dust and the dirt of the earth."

"Well," the scientist said, "give me time and we can do that too." And as he was speaking to God, the scientist reached down to get a handful of dirt to take with him to analysis and study.

To which God replied, "No, no, no, my dear child, you get your own dirt!"

So everything, absolutely everything came from him. He is the God of the universe. The God of all creation, the God to whom we owe not only our very existence, but also the existence of everything and anything. God is the absolute and supreme Creator. Yes indeed, we do have a very majestic and awesome God, so it is almost frightening then to think that it is toward that God that we have the audacity and the arrogance to develop an attitude of apathy.

But even as majestic and as powerful as our God is, he is also a God of Love. He is a loving God who takes a very personal interest in every aspect of our lives. He is a God whose love for us is so immense, and whose interest in us is so personal, that he had sent to us His only begotten Son, Our Lord and Savior Jesus Christ.

In the third chapter of the Gospel of John, Jesus said to Nicodemus, "Yes, God so loved the world that he gave his only Son." (John 3:16a) Our God loves us so much that he sent his only Son into this world of ours, the world that he had created for us, to be one like us in all ways but sin.

Yes, we have a God who desires a personal and

intimate relationship with us. But not only once we get to heaven. He also desperately wants one with us while we are here on this earth. We have a God who yearns for us to have a full and abundant life while we are in this world. In the tenth chapter of the Gospel of John, Jesus personally assured us of this fact when he said, "I came that they may have life and have it to the full." (John 10:10b) And to think that this is the God towards whom we have the arrogance to develop an apathetic attitude.

In the book *The Yellow Brick Road*, William J. Bausch describes spiritual apathy as "a spiritual dryness, a deadness of the soul." [5] Using this definition, one would assume that an attitude of apathy is the result of a soul not being nurtured or fed in order to help grow, mature, and flourish. The result is a dryness that could produce an ultimate deadness. Nothing can survive unless it is nurtured and fed. Faith that is allowed to lie dormant without any attention given to it will soon wither and fade away into a lifeless state.

But Bausch also describes the attitude of apathy that many of us experience today as being an attitude of the *"whatever"* syndrome or the *"cool"* syndrome. This is when we develop an attitude of arrogance toward our God. This is an attitude whereby we think of ourselves as being almost "too smart," too rich," "too popular," "too good looking," "too busy," "too important," or "too intelligent."

Toward God and religion we have developed an arrogant attitude of "whatever." We are not mad at, nor have we turned away from God. But rather we have slowly faded away because of our attitude of "whatever." Because of our "whatever" attitude toward God, we have slipped further and further away from a relationship with him, and even worse than that, we have slipped into the attitude which seems to say, "It's just no big deal!"

But it is a big deal to God. Numerous times throughout Sacred Scripture, we are told of the importance he places on having a meaningful and passionate relationship with us. In the Book of Exodus we are told, "You shall not worship any other god, for the Lord is 'the Jealous One'; a jealous God is he." (Exodus 34:14) In addition, in the fourteenth chapter of the Gospel of Luke, Jesus uses the analogy of salt losing its flavor to one losing the zeal and zest of their faith. Jesus said, "Salt is good, but if salt loses its flavor what good is it for seasoning. It is fit for neither the soil nor the manure heap; it has to be thrown away." (Luke 14:34–35) Like salt that loses its flavor, once we lose the passion for our faith, it can become lifeless and flavorless, and we develop an attitude of apathy—an attitude of "whatever."

In the Book of Revelation, Jesus uses even stronger words to stress his point on this issue when he said, "I know your deeds; I know you are neither hot or cold. How I wish you were one or the other–hot or cold! But because you are lukewarm, neither hot nor cold, I will spew you out of my mouth!" (Revelation 3:15–16)

God has no time for our arrogant attitude of

apathy. Regarding those with such a lukewarm apathetic attitude of "whatever," he says he will spit us
out of his mouth. He says it would even be better if
we were totally cold rather than just have the "Oh
well" attitude. To quote Radar O'Riley in one of the
M.A.S.H. TV episodes when he was speaking to
Hawkeye Pierce, who was acting as sort of a know-
it-all, *"Whooo do you think youuu are anyway?"*

But because of the great love he has for us, he
respects our freedom and has given to us the gift of
free will, thus allowing us to make our own choices,
or own decisions, and the freedom to form our own
attitudes. Because we are permitted by our God to
make our own choices and develop our own arrogant
attitudes toward him, we often find ourselves losing
sight of what the "Objective" of life really is.

Earlier I stated that the "Objective" of our lives
would have no validity until we can first give full and
undisputable validity to its author. We must comprehend the very basic fact that God is God, because
God is God. And our God, who is God, is the Creator
of everything, including you and me. And it is to that
God that we owe everything that we are, and everything that we can be. And the more deeply we can
comprehend that very basic fact of life, then and only
then will we come to the realization that our God is
not only the author of the "Objective of our Lives,"
He is the objective of our lives. For it is through him,
with him, and in him that we have our very being, for
He alone is God.

It is when we fail to keep God as the Objective

of our life that we tend to get ourselves into trouble. We begin to look only at our temporary success to obtain happiness. We want to live our lives according to our own personal agenda, and that is when the wheels of life can come off. That is when the chaos of life can become the norm in our lives. But God did not intend for our lives to be such. His intention and his desire from when he first created us as his most prized creation was that life for us here on earth could and should be happy, and that our happiness on this earth would prepare us for our everlasting life of happiness awaiting for us in the paradise of Heaven. In Isaiah we are told, "For thus says the Lord, The creator of the heavens, who is God, The designer and maker of the earth who established it, Not creating it to be a waist, but designing it be lived in: I am the Lord, and there is no other." (Isaiah 45:18)

God did put everything in place so this world that he created could be *lived* in without all the chaos that sometimes surrounds life in our world today. God wants us to "Live" life and not just to exist. He wants us to "Experience" life and all the gifts and treasures he has put on this earth for our enjoyment for the glory and praise of his name. He wants us to be "Happy" in this life. Those who are depressed and angry and constantly down in the dumps cannot serve him in the way he desires for us, his servants, to build his Kingdom.

God created the good things in this world for his people who keep a focus on him as the one and only "Objective" of their life. In Scripture we hear:

"Every worthwhile gift, every genuine benefit comes from the Father of the heavenly luminaries, who cannot change and who is never shadowed over." (James. 1:17)

All the tools are there for us to have a good, productive, meaningful, successful, and happy life in this world, while still keeping our minds focused on a passionate relationship with our God as the "Objective" of our lives.

During the remainder of this book, we will explore the tools that will enable us to work with the grain of the world, as it exists today, while still keeping our focus on our "Objective." We will discuss ways to avoid swimming against the current of the world, as it is so much easier to go with the current, provided we are in our own canoe, and we are controlling where the canoe will end up. Gandhi said it so well when he said, "Happiness is when what you think, what you say, and what you do are in harmony."

So now let's move on to discuss the tools you will need to be better able to put together your *Life's Strategic Plan*. Keeping in mind these words:

Trust & Confidence

"If anyone of you is without wisdom,
let him ask it from the God who gives gen-
erously and ungrudgingly to all,
and it will be given to him.
Yet he must ask in faith, never doubting,
for the doubter is like the surf tossed
and driven by the wind.
A man of this sort, devious and
erratic in all that he does,
must not expect to receive anything from the Lord."

(James 1:5–8)

chapter five

The Vision

So now that we have the objective of our lives firmly fixed in our minds, it is time to begin putting together the plans and specifications for our *Life's Strategic Plan*. We begin this task by first determining what we would like for our lives to be. What is it that we are driven toward? What is it that that we are working and striving for in life? And most importantly, how we can achieve that which we are after, while still keeping our eyes and mind firmly fixed and focused on the "Objective" of our lives? And our "Objective," of course, is our God.

In this land of unlimited opportunity in which we live, we have a tendency to feel the need, if not even the obligation, to live our lives in the fast lane. We want it all. However, the problem is that few of us really know what we really mean when we say that we want "it all."

If you were asked to make a list of everything you would like to accomplish, achieve, and have in life, what would your list include? Naturally for each of us, our list would be as varied as we are as individuals. However, in all likelihood there would be many items that we would all have in common.

The chances are that if we could "have it all," our primary list would include the fundamentals of success, riches, and happiness. The problem that arises, however, is in our definition of what we really mean when we say we want success, riches, and happiness. So another step we need to take before we can begin to meticulously put together our *Life's Strategic Plan* is that we need to know what it is that we want our lives to be, for the first rule in establishing any goal in life is that one must first have a clear *vision* of the goal.

If I get into my car and begin to drive, solely because I have a desire to go somewhere without a known destination, chances are I will never arrive anywhere of purpose. On the contrary, if I am currently at point "A" and my goal is to get to point "B," and if I have a clear vision of my intended destination, chances are fairly good that I will get there. For as we quoted Dr. Henry Kissinger previously, "If you don't know where you are going, every road will get you nowhere."

Author, actor, and TV celebrity Ben Stein once said, "The indispensable first step to getting the things you want out of life is this: Decide first what you want." Most of us really do not know what it is that we want from life. We may think we do, but studies over the years have proven the opposite. The fact is that most people are chasing a dream they cannot even describe with any degree of detail or vision. Most of us, at the very best, are chasing only a concept of what we would *like* for our lives to be. We find ourselves chasing after a life we only *wish* could be ours. It's a well-proven fact that most people go through life without identifying and establishing their goals, much less having a clear vision of the outcome of their plan. The reason for this is that most folks simply cannot describe what it is that they want their life to be. Most people simply do not have a vision of the life they would like to have. Until we have that clear vision, we will be unable to formulate a precise and clear-cut blueprint for our *Life's Strategic Plan*.

To illustrate the necessity of having a vision, I would like to share with you a little story. The story is about a hound chasing a fox through the woods, and it goes like this:

As the hound ran after the fox with all his mighty effort, he barked and yapped and howled as most hounds do. Upon hearing the hound yapping and howling, a second hound joined in on the chase adding to the barking, yapping and howling. Soon, a third hound also joined in on the chase, and then a fourth.

Now the fox was a crafty old guy and was successful in dodging and ducking in all sorts of ways. In addition, he was also quite fast - fast enough, in fact, that the hounds could not keep up, much less catch him. Soon the fourth hound, all tired and all tuckered out, dropped off and quit the case, followed closely by the third hound. Finally, after a little more chasing, barking, yapping, and howling, the second hound also called it quits, leaving only the original hound, seemingly with energy to spare, still chasing after the fox. With full determination he continued his yapping and howling and barking with all his might.

Now witnessing this event was a young lad and his father. The young lad asked his father, "Why is it that the fourth hound, although starting in the chase much later, was the first to fall out of the race. Then the third hound and finally the second hound also dropped out, leaving only the first hound still chasing the fox, and still with so much energy and determination?"

The father explained to his young son, "You see, only the first hound had seen the fox. Although the other three knew full well the fox was somewhere ahead of them, but they had not seen him. Only the first hound had the vision. And that vision is what gave that first hound the energy and determination he needed to keep up the chase."

To accomplish great things in life, one must first have the vision. Without the vision, a person is apt to become frustrated, run out of energy, and lose the desire for the chase.

Donald Trump had a vision. Bill Gates had a vision. Danny Thomas had a vision when he began St. Jude's Children's Hospital. Mother Teresa had a vision as she worked tirelessly to help those who were lost, forgotten, and dying in the streets of Calcutta. So did Dorothy Day as she worked day and night to provide a home for the homeless. And because each of these people had a vision, their efforts made a difference not only in their lives, but also in the lives of countless others. Their clear vision gave each of them the ability to succeed where others, without the vision, could only have hoped for a mere fraction of their success.

But the necessity for a clear vision in life is not reserved for the rich and powerful or the famous people of the world. Vision is equally important for all of us everyday folks as well. Helen Keller once said, "The greatest tragedy in life is people who have sight but no vision."

Having a vision determines the difference between the postal carrier who knows everyone on his route by name and whistles while he works, and the one is a constant complainer that life is just not fair, and nobody ever gives him a break.

Having a vision can determine the difference between the teacher who challenges her students and makes a positive difference in their lives, from the one who considers their vocation as "just a job, just a paycheck."

Napoleon Hill once said, "Cherish your visions and dreams, as they are the children of your soul; the blueprints of your ultimate achievements." Having a vision in life enables one to clearly see the fruit of their dreams and efforts. Having a vision will also assist an individual in recognizing many of the pitfalls and obstacles that may be encountered along the way. For if they can be recognized beforehand, they will be much easier to maneuver around than if they come upon a person by surprise.

Having both a *vision* and a *dream* are necessary. While it is possible for a person to have a dream without a vision, it is *not* possible for one to have a vision without first having a dream. The dream is the desire in one's heart, whereas the vision is the faith and confidence that the dream can and will become a reality. One who has vision can, with full faith and confidence, visualize the dream as becoming a reality. Jesus teaches us of this important fact of life in Scripture when he told us, " . . . if you have faith the size of a mustard seed, you could say to this sycamore, 'Be uprooted and transplanted into the sea,' and it would obey you." (Luke 17:6) Then in the Gospel of Matthew, Jesus even makes his point even stronger when he tells us, " . . . believe me, if you trust and do not falter, not only will you do what I did to the fig tree, but if you say to this mountain, 'Be lifted up and thrown into the sea,' even that would happen." (Matthew 21:21)

It's faith that gives a person the ability to move mountains. It's faith that gives a person the ability to see the reality of the dream in vivid detail.

For example, a person with only a dream but no faith or vision is someone who may dream of success, yet cannot define what success means to them. Such a person will flounder through life in a state of constant frustration, as they will not often recognize the success they may be after, even if by some remote chance they do obtain it.

In contrast, a person who combines faith and a vision with their dream cannot only describe in vivid detail what success means to them, but equally as important, they can provide a blueprint containing their detailed plans and specifications explaining *how* they intend to achieve their success. Before we can have our vision, we first need to be able to describe it as we see it. For our *Life's Strategic Plan* to be effective, we need these three important ingredients—the dream, the vision and the faith.

In the next three chapters we will discuss in more detail each the three areas of life that most of us seek after, those areas that we tend to dream about the most - *success, riches,* and *happiness.* By this discussion, we will be able to effectively determine our understanding of each, and with that information in hand we can then successfully design our *Life's Strategic Plan.*

Faith and Vision

As Jesus entered Capernaum, a centurion
approached him with this request:
"Sir, my serving boy is at home in bed
paralyzed, suffering painfully."
He said to him, "I will come and cure him."
"Sir." The centurion said in reply,
"I am not worthy to have you under my
roof, just give an order and my boy will get
better. I am a man under authority myself
and I have troops assigned to me.
If I give one man the order. 'Dismissed,' off he goes.
If I say to another, 'Come here,' he comes.
If I tell my slave, 'Do this,' he does it"
Jesus showed amazement on hearing
this and remarked to his followers,
"I assure you, I have never found
this much faith in Israel.
To the centurion Jesus said, "Go home, *It
shall be done because you trusted.*"
That very moment the boy got better.

[Emphasis added]
(Matthew 8:5–10; 13)

chapter six

Success

In this chapter we will discuss our *success* and how that success may either bring us closer to, or lead us further away from our God, who is the "Objective" of our lives.

Several years ago a young college student who was a close friend to one of our sons, and whose family is also a good friend of our family, died as the result of a tragic accident. In preparation for the funeral service, it was decided that in order to accommodate the number of people that were anticipated to attend, the wake service that was to be held on the evening prior to the funeral was moved from the funeral home to the family's parish church. Both events were packed with people beyond capacity.

As the memory of Doug was shared by so many, a thought entered my mind: Isn't it the hope of every parent, as they hold a newborn infant child for the very first time, that this precious little child will be a success in life and make their mark on the world that he or she has just entered into? I could not help but think of the impact and the mark this young man had made on the lives of so many in the short 19 years that he was on this earth. He accumulated no massive wealth; he had no recognizable power-ful position; and was awarded no front page, news breaking prestigious honors. But yet I could not help but think that even in the midst of the gut-wrenching pain of loss and sorrow that his parents were expe-riencing at that time of their lives, how very proud they were of this young son of theirs. For many kings and princes would have been so fortunate as to attain the success in life Doug had by touching the lives of so many in the way he had in only a short 19 years.

As I was thinking about the life of this young man and the mark that he made on his world, I could not help but draw a contrast between his life and that of the life of Howard Hughes. Now why the name of Howard Hughes entered my mind I could not tell you. But Howard Hughes, as is well known, was a man who was successful even almost beyond all standards of the world. He had accumulated more wealth and riches than he could ever count or spend. He had power and influence that only a handful of people would ever attain. He was awarded numerous prestigious honors and awards in his lifetime. And yet, even with all he had accomplished and attained in life, it was of little or no benefit to him in the end.

We have all read accounts explaining how the last years of his life were pure hell for him. It has been reported that he became very paranoid. He trusted almost no one. He withdrew into total seclu-sion. His fear of everything from the food people would serve him to even the fear of someone cutting his fingernails became a neurotic obsession for him.

He died alone. Not a single person who loved him as a child of God was at his bedside when he drew his last breath. It's been reported that those who were in control of his life were only interested in the wellbeing of his massive financial empire.

Now I am in no way degrading or wanting to demean the life of Howard Hughes in the slightest. In addition, there is always the real danger in speaking about the life of someone in light of the fact that we really do not know what was in his heart. That we must leave for the wisdom and love of God. But I draw the comparison between the life of a young 19 year old college student who left no material fortune or fame behind, to that of a multi-billionaire, and I would ask you, from what we do know, which of the two would you conclude had the most successful life?

Based on the standards of the world, Mr. Hughes was successful in business, but Doug, a young 19 year old college student, found success in life. Howard Hughes forgot one of the basic rules of life as defined by Robert Louis Stevenson when he said, "Perpetual devotion to what a man calls his business is only to be sustained by perpetual neglect of many other things."

Howard Hughes was obsessed with the success of his business enterprises. So obsessed, in fact, that he forgot to have a life along the way. On the surface anyway, it would appear that his life, as defined by Stevenson, was defined by the *"Perpetual Devotion"* to his business, rather than on keeping his eyes fixed and focused on the God who should have been the objective of his life.

While each of us may describe success and what it means to us in many different ways, I think it is somewhat safe to say that most of us would fall into the trap of describing success in the way that Howard Hughes did. We would describe it as a matter of "*doing*" rather than a matter of "*being*." Most of us would use *accomplishments* of life as a measuring stick for our success, rather using the *type* life that is *lived* as being the measuring stick. But as Zig Ziglar stated, "The things that count most in life are the things that can't be counted."

Now before we go any further, I would like to make one point clear. I am not against a person being successful in life. In fact, I am just the opposite. I am a promoter of success. It is my firm opinion that God gave us our gifts and talents to be used. It is further my position that a person can offend God just as much by not using the gifts and talents they were blessed with as one can by abusing them.

However, when it comes to the topic of success, there are two types of people that often get themselves into trouble, and as a result, they generally miss the entire point of the blessings and gifts that God has bestowed upon them.

The first type is the successful person who thinks that because of their level of success and achievements, they are somehow more valuable and or better than someone who has not achieved success, or at least success to the degree that *they* have achieved. They feel they are somehow more deserving than those who are less successful. People who develop their talents and yet also have these superiority attitudes are what can be called "abusers" of the gifts and talents with which God has blessed them.

The second type of person is the person who feels that they are not successful in life due *totally* to the fault of someone who is successful. This is the person with the attitude that God has made only a limited supply of the good things in this world. And whatever they don't have, it's because someone already has it, and because someone else has it, now they can't get it, and life or the system is stacked against them, and it just isn't fair. What is really ironic, and almost downright funny, is that these folks also fall into the same trap as the successful person. They also feel they are somehow more valuable, or better, or certainly more righteous than a person who has gained a degree of success. They also feel they are more deserving than those who are successful. These are the people who typically fall into the category of being what I call the "non-users" of the gifts and talents they have been blessed with.

In this world we live in, in this land of freedom and opportunity, we can find people at both ends of the success spectrum. On one end, we find the "abusers" and at the other end we find the "non-users." On one end is the *"gainers,"* and at the other end we find the *"complainers."*

The good indication as to whether a person becomes a gainer or a complainer lies primarily in two factors. The first factor lies in the "What." What is it that a person does in life to utilize the gifts and talents they have been blessed with? The second factor lies in the "How." How does a person use the gifts and talents they have been blessed with? The "What" factor will often determine the complainers, and the "How" factor will often determine the gainers.

The "What" Factor

One of the first important decisions that we all have to make on the threshold of adulthood lies in the "What" factor. Just *what* type of work or profession should I be in? *What* is God calling me to do in life? *What* am I best suited for? *What* type of work, profession or career will give me the most satisfaction and fulfillment in life? *What* can I do that will make me feel successful in life?

When giving consideration to "what" we do on the roadway to our desired success in life, it is important to realize that God leaves this as a matter of a free choice that he wants for each of us to make on our own. We can serve God equally as well, and our value to him and his love for us will be the same regardless if we are a renowned scientist who develops a life saving drug, or the circus clown who can bring a belly laugh to a small child. American tennis champ Arthur Ashe, Jr. once said, "Success is a journey, not a destination. The doing is usually more important than the outcome." So it is with our chosen careers in life.

But that does not mean that the renowned scientist should be the circus clown, or vice versa. I have seen scientists that, because of the personality God had blessed them with, could not even get as much as a chuckle out of a small child, much less be a successful circus clown. Likewise, a circus clown, in all probability, would not be very successful at developing a life saving drug, regardless of how many endless hours they spent in the lab.

God has two main desires for us while we are on this earth. The first is for us to keep him as the primary objective in life. The second is for us to find happiness and fulfillment in our daily life. Chances are that neither of his desires will come about if the "what" we are doing in this life does not coincide with the gifts and talents he has blessed us with. Author and a host of PBS "American Experience," David McCullough, said, "Real success is finding your lifework in the work that you love."

As a general rule, those who are the most unhappy and dissatisfied with what they are doing in life are usually those who are not fully utilizing the gifts and talents they have been blessed with.

In a poll conducted by the Gallup Organization in August of 2002, it was reported that in the age group of 18–29, only 39% state that they are completely satisfied with the job or profession they are in. For ages 30–40, that percentage increases only slightly to still just 42%. Even for the age group of 50–64, the group that is approaching the age of retirement and has been working for upwards to 40 years or more, still only 49% - less than half - feel completely satisfied with the type of job or profession they are in. [6]

Think of the reality of those numbers for a minute. For young men or women in the age group of 18–29, when their work and careers should be still fresh and exciting, over 60% of them feel less than fully happy with what they are doing. Why is that? Could the answer be in the very basic fact that they are in a job, profession or career that they are not wired for? Could it be that they have decided to settle for "just a job." Based on those statistics, one can only conclude that more than 50% of those in the American workplace today are unhappy with what they are doing. That is a national tragedy.

So often we pick a job or profession based on either what it pays, or we pick the one that we think we will have the best chance of getting hired for. Most people pick their jobs or careers based on the *"doing"* rather than on the *"being,"* and that is really sad. If you ask people the question, "If you could have any job in life that you wanted, what would that be?" you would discover that the majority would not name the job or profession they are currently in.

A true mechanic is happiest when he can lie under a car and get his hands dirty. Put him in a suit and tie and set him in front of a computer all day, and you will have one miserable person to live with. He would be miserable and frustrated with life, even if you were to pay him double what he may now be earning. And likewise, take the computer genius and have them change roles with the mechanic, and we would only end up with yet another miserable person, regardless of how much more you would pay him.

While there are many different avenues for the mechanic or the computer genius to use their individual gifts and aptitudes in this world, if they are not utilized in the way God had intended, chances are that fulfillment and contentment in a career will not be found. But how many mechanics in this country do we have sitting in front of a computer simply because of what it pays, or worse yet, because the company was hiring. And how many computer geniuses do we have lying under a car for the same reasons. Both professions are honorable, provided the right people are in them.

Dr. Albert Schweitzer once said, "Success is not the key to happiness. Happiness is the key to success. If you love what you are doing, you will be successful."

God's desire is for each of us to be happy in the work we do, and he has wired each of us in such a fashion that unless we use the gifts and talents with which he has blessed us, we will not be totally happy, nor will we find fulfillment or satisfaction in what we do, regardless of how much money we may be earning. It is very difficult for us to keep our focus on God as our objective if our life is miserable and frustrating because of how we are spending almost one-third or more of our lives.

And when a person is miserable and unhappy with what they are doing in life due to the lack of satisfaction or fulfillment they receive, they often fall into the group called the "complainers." We can find these folks in all levels of society and in every profession. We find these people working in our factories, our offices, our shops and restaurants, our hospitals, and yes, even in our churches and synagogues. Good people, making life miserable for both themselves and others simply because they are not doing in life what God has truly wired them for. Good people who could and would serve the Kingdom of God so much better if they would only use the gifts and talents that God had so blessed them with.

Yet we need to realize, of course, that we all have obligations and commitments to meet. We may have a family to support and bills to pay. And in all likelihood, it would be doubtful if it would be responsible to simply wake up one morning and decide to quite your job as a scientist so you can become a circus clown.

But on the other hand, if you're unhappy and miserable in what you are doing, chances are that you are taking that frustration and dissatisfaction home with you. Because of that, odds are fairly good that your family would rather have a happy clown to live with than a grumpy, grouchy and constantly complaining scientist. Not to mention how much happier your present co-workers would be if you would simply run away and join the circus.

The question and the discernment of what to do in life in order to fully utilize the gifts and talents with which you have been blessed is not something to be taken lightly. It's serious business. It truly makes a difference if one can keep their eyes and mind fixed and focused on the God who is the Objective of our lives.

The discernment of the call in life has been the point of considerable prayerful meditation by even many saints throughout the ages. St. Francis of Assisi, the founder of the Franciscans, spent considerable time in prayer and meditation on the discernment of the will and the call of God. St. Ignatius, the founder of the Jesuit Order, wrote extensively his *"Rules of Discernment"* for just that purpose.

In her book entitled *Faithful Listening,* Joan Mueller states that the Ignatius Rules are, "a guide by which Christians might discern whether the inner and outer movements that are a part of their lives are moving them toward greater love of God, neighbor and the world or edging them toward isolation and apathy." [7]

The "what" you do in life, therefore, is vital. Take an inventory of the gifts and talents with which God has blessed you, and then choose a career or profession where you will look forward to getting out of bed each and every morning and using those gifts to give thanks and praise to the God, who is the true objective of your life.

If your current job or profession does not provide that for you, then it is important for you to understand that you not only have the freedom and the right, but you also have an obligation to the God who blessed you with your gifts and talents, to take whatever *responsible* steps are necessary to change what you are doing. To make that change might require additional education, a change in lifestyle, or some planning and time to get everything in place. But as Mark Twain once said, "Plan for the future, because that's where you are going to spend the rest of your life."

True success in life is present, not based on the amount of money one earns or the position that is held, but rather when what you are doing causes you to move toward greater love of God, neighbor, and the world because you are doing what he has wired you for, and because of that, you enjoy what you're doing.

Earl Nightingale put it this way, "We are at our very best, and we are happiest when we are fully engaged in work we enjoy on the journey toward the goal we've established for ourselves. It gives meaning to our time off and comfort to our sleep. It makes everything else in life so wonderful, so worthwhile."

The "How" Factor

Running on a parallel track next to the "What" factor is the "How" factor. I say a parallel track, for one is neither ahead of nor behind the other. Both factors can prevent one from keeping their eyes and minds fixed on their God as the objective of their life.

The "how" factor relates to how we approach and how we do the "what" we do in life. One who is adversely affected by the "how" factor is one who has found their true calling in life. They are the person who cannot wait to get out of bed most every morning and go to a job or profession they love.

This is the scientist who is doing what he is doing because he is good at it.

This is the mechanic who is doing what he is doing because that is what he really wants to do, and he finds a since of therapeutic gratification in the grease and dirt he finds himself in daily.

This is the circus clown who finds complete fulfillment in bringing a belly laugh to the little child.

This is the computer genius that finds complete satisfaction in the fruits of his labor.

Now on the surface one might ask, "How can there be anything wrong with anyone who enjoys their work? How can there be any negativity to a person who finds fulfillment and satisfaction in their job or profession because they are good at it, and they are doing what they really want to do, because they have been wired to do exactly what they are doing?" Naturally, it goes without saying that there is absolutely nothing wrong with it, *provided* that the job or profession is kept in the perspective that God had meant it to be. The adverse affect of the "how" factor is when we become almost obsessed with our job or profession. The adverse affect of the "how" factor comes into play when one becomes so obsessed with what they are *doing* in life that they forget to have a life along the way.

These are the "gainers" of the world. These

people become obsessed with gaining more of whatever it is that their job or profession can offer. For some gainers, what they are looking to gain more of is money. For other gainers it could be a matter of power, prestige, or a position of honor. Yet for others, they could be obsessed with the mere sense of accomplishment. The reason behind the cause for the obsession, or even what the obsession is, really doesn't matter. Either way, the obsession will prevent us from keeping our eyes and minds fixed on the God who is the Objective of our lives.

In the sixth chapter of Matthew, Jesus said, "No man can serve two masters. He will either hate one and love the other or be attentive to one and despise the other. You cannot give yourself to God and money." (Matthew 6:24). It makes no difference what the riches are that we become obsessed with. Be it money, power, position, prestige, the feeling of accomplishment, or even the adrenalin one gets from the excitement of the chase.

In and of itself, there is absolutely nothing wrong with enjoying, or even having a sense of passion for what we are doing. When we can enjoy and experience a sense of fun and excitement in our work, that makes God smile. He wants us to enjoy the gifts he gave us. It is through our enjoyment of life that we help God build his Kingdom out of loving service rather than out of grudging labor.

But even more than that, he wants to remain our God. He wants to remain the "Objective" of our lives. When we become obsessed with our accomplishments, the "Objective" of our lives changes. Instead of our God being our "Objective," what we accomplish, and even we ourselves, become the objective of our lives. That works for a while, but sooner or later it catches up with everyone. One way or another, it will catch up with absolutely everyone.

To exemplify my point, I would like to share with you a story about two true to life friends of mine. Each came from very modest beginnings. Each was raised in typical, Midwestern, small town communities. Both entered the business world about the same time and both became what by most standards would be considered as very financially successful individuals. But that is where the two part ways.

For my first friend, once he tasted the sweetness of success, he became obsessed with it. He had to have more. It was an addiction that he craved every waking hour. He developed a philosophy that if it was good for his business and his success, it then had to be good. And that philosophy took over his life. Everything he did and became was the result of it.

A few years ago I met up with him for lunch during the week between Christmas and New Years. The topic turned to the activities of the holidays, and I asked him if his kids were all home for Christmas. "No," he said, "My wife and I had a very relaxing day." He said, "A couple of the kids called, but they were all busy on Christmas." But he said they would stop over sometime during the holidays. He said, "I spent most of the day getting things ready for my year-end taxes and my wife spent most of her day surfing the Internet looking for decorating ideas. The day was a real quiet and quite relaxing for both of us."

As my friend was sharing with me what his Christmas was like, my heart really went out to him, because what he said was one thing; how I interpreted what he said was another. The following is my interpretation of what he was really saying:

My third wife and I spent Christmas alone without my kids or her kids coming over. They'll all come over sometime during the holiday season to pick up the gifts we bought for them, but we no longer have a sense of a feeling of home, so they are going elsewhere for the day. So I spent the day doing what I like to do better than anything else; I worked on my financial affairs. And my third wife, why she spent the day in another room with her nose buried in the computer trying to find yet something else she could buy.

For this friend of mine, as is always the case, it caught up to him. Sooner or later, and in one way or another, it catches up to everyone. He lost his focus on what should have been the true objective of his life. He became obsessed and addicted to material things and his own accomplishments, and in the process of making a successful career, he failed to have a life.

On the other hand, for my second friend, things are just the opposite. Now while I have no concrete proof, it is my assumption—and I think it is a fairly safe assumption—that the financial net worth for this second friend far exceeds that of my other friend. But here is the real difference.

My second friend has virtually never taken his eyes off of his God, who is the true "Objective" of his life. On one morning of each and every week, he meets with a group of other Christian businessmen who support each other in all the trials and tribulations of both life and business. Together they support each other much like the support of an AA group, so that even when the clouds get the darkest and the road gets the roughest, they remind each other of the true "Objective" of life. Together they help each other to keep their eyes and minds fixed and focused on God. And that is just one example. He is also involved in his church and offers leadership to several local charitable and civic organizations. He is married to his high school sweetheart and together they have five children. The other day I ran into him and with a smile from ear to ear he proceeded to tell me that he retired about six months ago, and has now turned the business over to his boys. Now he and his wife, hand in hand, are planning to travel and see the world together.

Keeping a focus on the God who is the true objective of life is no guarantee that one will be successful and gain riches, wealth, power, and prestige, but neither does it prevent it. In the Fifth Chapter of the Book of Ecclesiastes we read,

"Here is what I recognize what is good: it is well for a man to eat and drink and enjoy all the fruits of his labor under the sun . . . Any man to whom God gives riches and property, and grants power to partake of them, so that he receives his lot and finds joy in the fruits of his toil has a gift from God." (Ecclesiastes 5:17–18)

When we enjoy what we are doing and are successful at it, God smiles, for through our work and in our success we give him glory.

But he also made it very clear in the Fifteenth Chapter of John that if we try to do it on our own, or if we take our focus off of him, that will not work for very long either, as Jesus told us, " . . . no more than a branch can bear fruit of itself apart from the vine, can you bear fruit apart from me. I am the vine, you are the branches. He who lives in me and I in him, *will produce abundantly*, for apart from me you can do nothing." [emphasis added] (John 15:4–5)

We give glory to God when we are doing what he has wired us for, and when we do what we do best. Then the real glory comes when we still keep our eyes and mind fixed and focused on him as the "Objective" of life.

As B.C. Forbes said so wisely, "Don't forget until it's too late that the business of life is not business, but living."

Gifts From God

There are different gifts but the same Spirit;
there are different ministries but the same Lord;
there are different works but the same God
who accomplishes all of them in everyone.
But it is the one and the same Spirit
who produces all these gifts,
distributing them to each as he wills"

(1 Corinthians 12:4–6; 11)

chapter seven

Riches & Other Good Things in Life

We have been blessed to live in the richest country on the face of the earth. In our country, most people who live in even the most modest and humble of surroundings and situations would be looked upon as living in the lap of luxury compared to so many in other parts of this world.

Yet even though we are living in the midst of all the gifts and treasures with which God has so blessed us, we still find ourselves in the situation whereby, *because* of the all the blessings we have, we find it hard to keep our minds fixed on our God as the Objective of our lives.

When it comes to the subject of the riches, pleasures, and treasures of life, people usually fall into one of two primary categories. The first are those who do not think they have enough, and the second are those who have too much. People can fall into either of these two categories *regardless* of the size of their paychecks, their bank accounts, the cars they drive, the homes they live in, or the jobs they hold.

As a general statement, the vast majority of us fall into the first category; we are the folks who do not think we have enough, regardless of how much we already have. Of course, it goes without saying, but we always experience the riches and pleasures in life on a basis of relativity. What one person may call a luxury, the next person will consider a necessity. The amount of money one person may consider as being wealthy, the next will consider as a mere pittance. The same can be said of any of the other gifts and treasures we receive from God, regardless of what they are.

Not only are things relative from one person to the next, but they also become relative even to us personally as we move through life. Possessions, positions and abilities that we may have once worked, hoped, and prayed for lose the romanticism after they are obtained and usually are soon taken for granted. Seldom will someone say, "I am completely satisfied with exactly what I have."

In a poll taken by the Gallup Organization in December of 2003, the results found that only 14% of Americans feel highly satisfied with the amount of money they earn, and less than half (46%) are satisfied with where they live. [8] And again, this is across the board, regardless of the size of one's paycheck or the size of home in which they live.

In the second category, we find those who have too much. And again, like the first, this also goes across the board and has nothing to do with the size of one's paycheck or the possessions or abilities they may have. These are the people who cannot responsibly handle what they have been blessed with. They tend to squander their gifts and treasures in ways that God had not intended for them to be used. They do so as follows: *1)* using their money, talents, or abilities only for personal gain or pleasure without any consideration of the needs of anyone else, or *2)* tending to hoard their gifts and treasures like that of the stereotype played by the comedian of old, Jack Benny—who portrayed someone who loved to admire all his wealth and possessions, yet he never wanted to share or part with any of it, or *3)* maybe even a bit worse than that of the Jack Benny type are the flaunters. These are the people who want to show off everything they have. They want to talk about and flaunt their money, possessions, talents and abilities, but that is as far as their sharing goes. They have a "look but don't touch, because it's mine" attitude toward everything with which they have been blessed. This last type of person typically feels that everything they have is due 100% to their own, self-obtained talents and efforts, and it is therefore their birthright to have what they have, and as such, they feel no need or obligation to share any of it with anyone, at any time, for any reason.

Although we all sometimes make mistakes and tend to misuse the blessings that God has given us, that does not mean we are wrong in going after them. There is absolutely nothing wrong with living the American dream and having the drive and desire to go after every inch that life has to offer. It is only when the accumulation of "possessions, positions and wealth" becomes the primary objective of our lives, rather than keeping our focus on our God who is to be our true "Objective," that we begin to miss the whole point of what this life is really all about. Only when we lose the focus on our true "Objective" of life does our striving for more becomes a wrong idea.

We live in a land that God has blessed with a great deal of abundance. As Americans, we have almost an inborn sense of the yearning for exploring new frontiers. As I stated above, the desire to improve our position in life is not necessarily a bad thing. The freedoms we enjoy with our form of government and the society that we have built grants to each and every one of us the guaranteed right to life, liberty, and the pursuit of happiness. Our country has been known for centuries as the land of opportunity and the land of unlimited frontiers. We can cite countless examples of people from every race, color, religion, sex, ethnic origin, and physical handicap that have become successful within their own right and in their chosen path of life. These are people who have explored new frontiers for their own pursuit of happiness.

Sam Walton began his retail career working as a sales clerk in a J.C. Penny Store in Des Moines, Iowa. Ray Crock, the founder of the McDonalds chain, began his career selling malted milk machines. Steve Jobs began Apple Computer out of his father's garage. Henry Ford began his career tinkering in the blacksmith shop on his dad's farm. Each of these individuals used the gifts and talents with which God had blessed them for their own personal pursuit of happiness.

The names of folks like Helen Keller, Colin Powell, Oprah Winfrey, Jimmy Carter, Charles Wang, and Ronald Reagan are only a mere hint of others who have achieved substantial success from very modest, if not even dire beginnings; all for their pursuit of happiness.

And these are only a few who are among the more well-known. Think of all the people whom you know personally who have become successful within their own right. People you know who succeeded against all odds. People who succeeded in spite of a physical handicap or racial, ethnic, gender or other barriers they had to overcome. These are the people who are living the American dream. In America, we believe that not only do we have a God-given right, but equally as important, we also have the vision and a faith in our ability to move between the social classes. That belief that we hold firm and sacred to our way of life is an important part of our national identity. It is part of what makes us the great county that we are. Indeed, we hold our right to our pursuit of happiness as being almost sacred to us.

God has immensely blessed this land of freedom and opportunity in which we live. As I stated in the last chapter, when we are successful in using the gifts and talents with which God has blessed us, we are certainly giving him reason to smile and be happy with us. For as long as we keep him as the "Objective" of life, there is no greater way to give him the praise and glory that He is due. There is no greater way to give him thanks than for us to successfully use the gifts and talents that he has given to us. St. Ireneus assures us that the glory of God is humans fully alive.

Throughout the Sacred Scripture we are reassured that blessings from God are to be cherished. We are given the assurance that he has also made all the good things of this world for *his* people. In the second Chapter of the Book of Ecclesiastes we hear this, "There is nothing better for man than to eat and drink and provide himself with good things by his labors. Even this, I realized, is from the hand of God. For who can eat and drink apart from him? (Ecclesiastes 2: 24–25)

Then in the fifth chapter of Ecclesiastes are these words of wisdom, "Here is what I recognize as good: it is well for a man to eat and drink and enjoy all the fruits of his labor under the sun . . . Any man to whom God gives riches and property, and grants power to partake of them, so that he receives his lot and finds joy in the fruits of his toil, has a gift from God." (Ecclesiastes 5:17–18)

God has revealed to us through Sacred Scripture that not only is it his desire for us to be successful in this life, but that he also desires that we enjoy the good things that he has given to us, and I stress these basic points of fact for two very important reasons.

The first reason is that I believe that part of the cause for the attitude of apathy toward God and religion for so many is the false impression that one cannot have success in life *plus* a quality relationship and a life of service to God at the same time. For all too many in our modern-day society, we totally miss the point as to the true meaning of a life of service to God. We have the false impression that there is a real conflict between our success in this world and keeping God as the objective of life. Because of the constant rhetoric of separation of church and state, we have assumed that we must keep God also separate from our business or professional lives. In actuality, we are serving God the best when we are successfully using the gifts and talents that we have received from him in all aspects of our lives. If being successful is the result of using the gifts and talents you have been blessed with, then it would only be an insult to God if you did not use those gifts to their fullest.

If God gave you the gift of leadership and you did not use those gifts to lead, you would be denying God the glory he deserves. Regardless of whether you're a politician, a businessperson, a teacher, a coach, a person in the military, a police officer, a pastor, or a parent, God gave you the gift of leadership for a purpose—He wants and expects you to use your gift.

If God gave you the gift of having a good business mind, he then expects you to use your gift to be as successful as you can. It's important to remember, however, that any financial rewards you receive from your success are only the scorecards as an indicator of how well you are using your gifts. The size of the financial rewards should never be construed or misinterpreted as to the "worth" or "value" you are as a person, especially in the eyes of God. It makes no difference to him if the amount that you earn is measured in hundreds, thousands, millions or billions. The amount you are able to earn is immaterial to him. What is important to God is what you do with what he has given you.

If God gave you the gift of an especially understanding heart—the gift of being able to be a good listener—then that is what God expects you to do, regardless of whether you do that as a high paid psychiatrist, a professional school teacher, a den mother or scout leader, or just a good friend.

God created each of us and put us on this earth at this particular time in the vastness of the history of creation for a very specific and important purpose. He blessed us with our special gifts for a very specific reason and purpose. In the first chapter of the Book of Jeremiah, God tells us, "Before I formed you in the womb I knew you, before you were born I dedicated you . . ." (Jeremiah 1:5) Then in the Book of Isaiah, God confirms to us once more just how important we are personally to him when he said, "The Lord called me from birth, from my mother's womb he gave me my name." (Isaiah 49:1b) Then in the Gospel of Matthew, Jesus reaffirms again just how important we as individuals are to him when he stated, "Are not two sparrows sold for next to nothing? Yet not a single sparrow falls to the ground without your Father's consent. As for you, every hair on your head has been counted; so do not be afraid of anything. You are worth more than an entire flock of sparrows." (Matthew 10:29–31)

Our God knows us very intimately, and just as His knowledge of us is very personal, so too, has he created us as individuals and given to each of us all our special gifts and talents. Serving God is a full-time job. He wants to be involved and glorified through *everything that we do in life*, not just for one hour on Sunday morning.

The Book of Proverbs tells us that, "The LORD has made *everything* for his own ends." [emphasis added] (Proverbs 16:4a) Wealth, riches, positions, talents and the good things of this world are not in conflict with God; rather, they exist for the purpose and glory of His Holy Name. It is only *how* we use these things that make them either good or evil.

The second reason I stress the point that God indeed wants for us to enjoy the good things of life is that we must come to the full and abiding realization and appreciation that it is God who is the giver of all good things. The more we are aware that God is the sole and exclusive provider of *everything* that is good—all our gifts, all our talents, all our treasures, all the good things we have in life—then it is to God that we can and will give the praise, honor, glory and thanksgiving that is due for all and everything we have.

The more we recognize that God is the sole and exclusive provider of all the good things we have, the less of a tendency we will have to claim personal and exclusive credit for our obtaining them.

The more we can come to realize that everything that is good comes to us from God, the less we tend to let our own personal ego get in the way of our relationship with both God and neighbor. The more we realize just how much God loves and provides for us, the less apathy we will have toward him, and the more we will involve him in every aspect of our lives. The more *He* will become the true "Objective" of our lives, the easier it will be for us to keep our focus on Him.

So once we have the firm realization that all good things do come to us as blessings from God, our next step is to recognize that, as with all good things, there comes a responsibility.

Regardless of the gift, the more valuable it is, the more responsibility that comes with it. We are reminded of this in the twelfth chapter of Luke when Jesus said, "When *much* has been given a man, *much will be required* of him. *More will be asked of a man to whom more has been entrusted.*" [emphasis added] (Luke 12:48b) The more gifts we are blessed with, the more responsibility we have to use them properly and for the glory of God's name. The more good things God puts in our lives, the more good God expects us to do with them.

The only way we can ever use any of our gifts from God responsibly is for us to adopt the spirituality of Christian Stewardship. Through serving others, we serve God. It is only through serving others that we become better people. It was Albert Schweitzer who said, "One thing I know. The only ones among you who are really happy are those who will have sought and found how to serve." St. Francis of Assisi put it very simply when he said, "For it is in giving that we receive."

Over the years the term "Stewardship" has become used and abused to the point that in many circles, it has lost its true meaning. For many of us, the word "Stewardship" is used today as a synonym for other words and phrases like tithing, charitable giving, pledging, or volunteering of time to the church or other charitable organization. While all of these actions can be considered as acts of steward-ship, they do not fully describe what Christian Stew-ardship really is all about.

Simply stated, Christian Stewardship is Spiri-tuality. It's a Spirituality of an inner knowledge and conviction that everything we have is from our lov-ing God. All our gifts, talents, time and treasures are the result of God's immense love for us. Everything is given to us for the Glory of God's name. Fur-ther, without God, we would have nothing. So since everything that is good comes to us from God, and since everything is for the glory of his name, and still further as we would have nothing if it were not from God, we then must also realize that everything that we have belongs to God, because God is God and the Creator of everything.

When we acknowledge that everything that we have is only on loan to us from God, we realize that we are only the stewards of his gifts. As stewards we have a serious responsibility to cherish them, to care for them, and to return them back to God with increase.

Once we develop a true Stewardship Spirituality, we tend to not only change our view of what we do with our gifts, but we also change our attitude of why it is that we share of our gifts and treasures in the first place. Instead of using terms like that of "Paying our debt to society" or "giving some of our hard earned money" or "paying to charity," we instead fully acknowledge from the onset that all that we have came to us from God as only a loan for us to use and cherish while we are here. Therefore, since everything is only a loan to us, rather than having the attitude that we are giving from what is ours, we face the reality that by sharing we are only being a good steward of the gifts and blessings he has given to us in the first place.

Stewardship is not simply an act, nor is it simply something that we do. Neither is Stewardship a program or a plan. *Stewardship is a way of life.* Stewardship is the spirituality of our recognition of just who God is, and the vital role that he has in everything that we have, and are, and can be in life. God expects us to be responsible stewards of everything he has given us, regardless of the size of our paycheck, our bank account, the home we live in, or the size or quantities of any other of the gifts he has given us.

I'm reminded of this little story of a child who

was awakened in the middle of the night by a bad thunderstorm. Startled by the racket of all the thunder and lightning, he cried out to his mother. In an attempt to comfort her child, she reassured him that he was safe and that everything would be okay, and that God was there to take care of him, even in the midst of the storm. "I know God is with me," he said, "but tonight I need a God with some skin on."

Having the Spirituality of Stewardship enables us to diligently do our daily work to the very best of our ability, and still fully enjoy what he has blessed us with. Because we know that in all that we do with what God has blessed us with and made us stewards over, we become for so many others "God with some skin on" by helping build of his Kingdom in so many ways.

Only after we fully adopt a true Spirituality of Stewardship for our lives will we begin to recognize that the good things of life are not just "things," but rather are to be recognized by us as being true blessings and gifts from God.

The Spirituality of Stewardship is an "Attitude of Gratitude" for all that we have been blessed with. With that "Attitude of Gratitude" we can then use and enjoy all that we have been given in a totally new light, for all our enjoyment of life becomes a true act of giving glory and praise to the God who is the giver of all good things and the "Objective" of our lives.

Only after we adopt a true Spirituality of Stewardship for our lives will we realize that we can never outdo the generosity of our God. The words of assurance to this fact came directly from the mouth of Jesus when he told us that, "Those who have, *will get more* until they grow rich . . ." [emphasis added] (Matthew 25:29a)

If you are a person who has a true, honest, and sincere Spirituality of Stewardship, then God has a sincere desire that you succeed within your own right and at the ability he gave to you. He wants you to be successful beyond all your imagination in whatever you do in life, and he will help you to do so, for he also knows you will be a good and dedicated steward of your treasures. In the Gospel of John, Jesus tells us that, "My Father has been glorified in your bearing *much* fruit . . ." [emphasis added] (John 15:8a)

For the person who lives a life with a true Spirituality of Stewardship, God really wants for them to enjoy *every* good thing of life that he has put at their disposal. When you have done all that you can do, and have enjoyed every blessing he has given you, and have been a good and responsible steward of the gifts of time, talents and treasures, he will then say to you,

"Come. You have my Father's blessings! Inherit the kingdom prepared for you from the creation of the world. For I was hungry and you gave me food, I was thirsty and you gave me drink. I was a stranger and you welcomed me, naked and you clothed me. I was ill and you confronted me, in prison and you came to visit me . . . I assure you, as often as you did it for one of my least brothers, you did it for me." (Mt 25:34b-36; 40)

When we adopt the Spirituality of Stewardship, our treasures, riches, pleasures, and all the good things we have in life become assets from God, not only on our own balance sheet, but equally so on God's balance sheet that he keeps for our personal account. With that advantage, it sure helps for us to be able put together our *Life's Strategic Plan.*

Trusting in the Lord's Generosity

. . . forget not my teaching, keep
in mind my commands;
For many days, and years of life
and peace they bring you.
Let not kindness and fidelity leave you;
bind them around your neck;
Then will you win favor and good
esteem before God and man.
Trust the Lord with all your heart, on
your own intelligence rely not;
In all your ways be mindful of him, and
he will make straight your paths.
Be not wise in your own eyes,
Fear the Lord and turn away from evil;
This will mean health for your flesh
and vigor for your bones.
Honor the Lord with your wealth and
first fruits of all your produce.
Then will your barns be filled with grain,
with new wine your vats will overflow.

(Proverbs 3:1–10)

Happiness

 In virtually every stage of life, the bottom-line motivation and the reason for almost everything we do is for the purpose of our pursuit of this thing we call *happiness*.

 The founding fathers of this great nation of ours held our right to the pursuit of happiness in such high degree that they placed it right alongside of our rights to life and liberty. To think about a life without happiness is almost incomprehensible. Our personal happiness affects all aspects of our lives. It affects the quality of the relationships we have with others, as well as the quality of our health and even life itself. When, for whatever reason we are unhappy, we find everything else much more difficult to deal with. Romance goes out of our love life. Toward our loved ones, our friends, and co-workers, we tend to recognize more of their faults and shortcomings. Our jobs become more of a drudge, our problems become less manageable, our hope for the future becomes more faded, and our ability to keep our eyes on our God as the "Objective" of our lives becomes more difficult. When we lose all happiness in our lives, we become disillusioned, discouraged, depressed, cynical, and pessimistic of almost every aspect of our lives, and most importantly, of God. When we lose happiness in life is when we begin to cry out as the Psalmist did when he said, "Will the Lord reject forever and nevermore be favorable? Will his kindness utterly cease, his promise fail for all generations? Has God forgotten pity? Does he in anger withhold his compassion?" (Psalm 77:8–10)

But, it is not God's will nor desire for us to be unhappy. His desire is for us to work and strive for happiness in this world so we can experience total and unsurpassable happiness in the next. In Psalm 128 we hear the Psalmist with a total change of heart and attitude, for by this time he found happiness again, so we hear him say, "Happy are you who fear the Lord, who walk in his ways! For you shall eat the fruits of your handiwork: happy shall you be, and favored!" (Psalm. 128:1–2)

Because happiness is so important to us not only as individuals but equally to us as a society, our founding fathers placed it in such a high importance as they did.

But what does that actually mean? When we in this land of unlimited opportunity are guaranteed the right to *"the pursuit of happiness,"* what does that really mean?

As adults we pursue our happiness by chasing all the dreams we have in life. We pursue happiness in the relationships we desire with our families and friends. We pursue happiness in our chosen jobs or careers. We pursue happiness in all the little pleasures and luxuries we are afforded in this great society of ours. We pursue happiness in the status we can attain among our peers and those in our social circles.

We are in such a constant pursuit of this thing we call happiness that we are almost pursued out. Our "pursuit of happiness" has turned into an "intense hunt for happiness," and our hunt has almost captivated our entire being. Between the schedules we keep, the activities we are involved in, the demands we place on our relationships, and the lifestyle we have grown accustomed to, we have pursued, hunted, chased after, and searched for happiness in everyone, everything and everywhere we can possibly think of—everywhere except for where we must be looking first—since the very first place we must look for our own personal happiness is within ourselves. While it goes without saying that our God is the true *source* of our happiness, yet we as individuals must take full responsibility for our own attitudes and actions that will produce the happiness we are pursuing.

While we can, in fact, find happiness "with" people, positions, or things, we do get ourselves into trouble, and our expectations of happiness are ruined when we begin to place the responsibility for our own happiness on other factors outside of ourselves. We get ourselves in trouble and our happiness is often ruined when we fail to take responsibility for our own happiness.

Let me give you an example of this. I can think of nothing that brings me greater happiness than having all of our kids along with their spouses, boyfriends and girlfriends, and all of our grandkids over for a Sunday afternoon backyard cookout on a nice summer day. But still, I must take responsibility for my own happiness. My own happiness must be first developed within myself. My experience of happiness with the family cookout would not exist if I would have the expectation that it is the responsibility of my family, or the event of the cookout, to *"make"* me happy.

Another example of this is that I find happiness every day with my position as an ordained cleric of the church and the work I do at my parish. However, that same happiness could not be experienced if I would expect that it is my position or my work that must *"make"* me happy.

Fr. John Powell summed up for us what our pursuit to happiness must entail in the title of his book, *Happiness Is an Inside Job.* [9] Our pursuit of happiness must begin within ourselves. Happiness is a matter of *"being."* It is not a matter of *"doing"* or "having." We will never achieve any degree of lasting happiness until we fully accept the basic fact that only we are totally responsible for our own personal pursuit of happiness.

God has blessed us with the love of family and friends for us to enjoy as a result of our happiness, but happiness itself is our responsibility. Other people, regardless of how much love or enjoyment they can *bring into* our lives, cannot "make" us happy. As Powell states it, "One of the most persistent and widely believed delusions is that one person can make another happy. You cannot confer on me the fullness of life. That has to be my choice." [10]

God blesses us with many of the good things in life to provide enjoyment as a result of our happiness, but our happiness becomes very shallow and short-term when our happiness is dependent upon the "things" in life. Dale Carnegie put it this way, "Remember that happiness doesn't depend on what you are or what you possess, but only on how you think."

Our happiness, to a great extent, will depend upon our actions, behaviors, and the attitudes that go into forming us as the individual people that we become.

So if we have the total responsibility for our own happiness, how much actual control do we, in fact, have in obtaining it? First, we need to realize that's a question that has been asked from the dawn of creation. No one, regardless of wealth, status, position, or physical or mental abilities, has total and/or absolute control in obtaining happiness. At best, any happiness we attain here on earth is only temporary. That is why our founding fathers termed it as the "pursuit" of happiness and not the "attainment" of happiness. Our pursuit of happiness is a lifelong endeavor. The greatest happiness we may experience here on earth is only a hint of the happiness we will experience in the presence of our God in his lasting Kingdom. St. Augustine said this of his pursuit of happiness, "My soul shall remain restless until I rest in the Lord."

However, there are certain things that we can and must do in life that will make a difference in the degree of happiness we experience. Our responsibility for our own happiness lies in the life we lead and who we are as individuals. A first big part of our responsibility is for each of us to be honest enough with ourselves to determine where we are in life, and what life has become. Only when we arrive at that honest discernment can we begin to change our lives in a new direction. Oliver Wendell Holmes, Jr., once said, "I find the great thing in this world is not so much where we stand, as in what direction we are moving." Only when we are moving in the right direction by taking responsibility for our own happiness can we then effectively put together our *Life's Strategic Plan.*

Establishing Priorities

One of our responsibilities in the quest for our pursuit of happiness is the need to establish proper priorities in life. Whether we establish the priorities of life or not, we still live our lives by a given set of priorities, even if subconsciously.

In his book *The Yellow Brick Road,* [11] William Bausch recounts the story former baseball player Harmon Killebrew told about his childhood. As the story goes, almost every day his father would take him and his brother out to the front lawn to practice baseball. He tells of his mother standing on the porch shouting to her husband that "all this base running was ruining the lawn." He said he remembers his father's reply: "Martha, we're not raising grass here. We're raising boys!"

That's establishing priorities. Most of us, when asked what our priorities in life are, could rattle off rather quickly what we think, or even wish our priorities in life were. However, what we say and the reality of our actions and attitudes may not always be the same.

In our pursuit of happiness, we need to establish proper priorities in every aspect of our lives. If we fail to establish priorities in our job or profession we may find ourselves unemployed. Unemployment seldom brings happiness.

If we fail to establish priorities in our personal life, we may find ourselves alienated in our relationships. Happiness certainly cannot be found there.

In our pursuit of happiness, each of us must make constant and honest discernment about what we truly have as the priorities in our lives. In doing so, we must remember that the priorities that are reflected in our actions do not always coincide with what we say or think is truly most important to us. Now at first reaction, one would surmise that this would be absurd and even irrational. Why in the world would we not place at our highest priorities that which we hold as being the most important in our lives? May I remind you again of the story told by the baseball player Harmon Killebrew. It would be inconceivable to think that for this mother, her two boys were not far more important to her than her lawn, yet her words indicated a different priority.

Most all of us have been guilty at one time or another of having misdirected our priorities. Times like those when we may have placed a higher priority on our careers than on loved ones who are truly more important to us. Times like those when we may have placed a higher priority on material possessions than on our relationships. Robert Louis Stevenson said, "Don't judge each day by the harvest you reap, but by the seeds you plant." The size and the quality of the harvest will be determined by the quality of the seed. The quality of the seeds we plant will be determined by the priorities we not only establish, but also hold firm in our actions and attitudes of life. It is in our actions and attitudes that we find our seeds.

It will be through the priorities we establish in our lives that we will find the happiness we are in pursuit of. The true priorities that we establish in life will, to a great extent, determine if we are able to keep our God as the "Objective" of our lives.

The Proverbial Rat Race

It has been said that time is a fixed income, and as with any income, the real problem facing most of us today is how to live successfully within our daily allotment.

In their book *Benedict's Way,* Lonni Pratt and Father Daniel Homan speak of the importance that time plays in our having a balanced and quality life. They state that,

Time is a holy thing. It is mysterious

and elusive while being practical and substantial. Because of the ways we measure time and because we coordinate our lives by the passage of time, we can sometimes have an artificial sense of managing time. The truth is that none of us can manage time any more than we can manage a hurricane or manage the seasons or manage God. The Holy One will not be held back by our trembling hands. [12]

Over the years I have attended no less than eight to ten different seminars and courses covering the topic of effective time management. Each course promised the ultimate wisdom as to how to manage time in the most effective and productive manor. I have used every conceivable style and type of appointment book on the market. In addition to the appointment books and calendars, I have also used the daily "Top Priority List," as well as the daily and weekly "To do" list.

These days I have also entered the age of semi-high tech. I now carry a PDA, which of course only means that I am now expected to have more information with me at all times. But the calendar . . . surprisingly, it still has only seven days in any given week, and only 24 hours in every single day! Technology has not yet been able to find a way to change that.

After all the courses and all the different appointment books and types of list and gadgets I have used over the years, I have finally come to the realization that the statement made by Pratt and Homan is correct, "none of us can manage time any more than we can manage a hurricane . . ." [13] When I really think about it, I had always known that the clock kept on ticking regardless of what I did or did not do. I also realized that regardless of the creativity I would try to put into my schedule, the day was no longer than the 24 hours God had given it. The sun came up and set according to God's schedule, not mine. What I also came to realize was that while I knew I could not make more time, the secret I really wanted to capture was how I could do more with the time I had. How could I jam more "stuff" into the 24 hours I had. I wanted to learn the secret of how I could do more, and get more accomplished in my already full, busy and sometimes even hectic and chaotic schedule.

Then some brain dead idiot came up with the term *"Multi-Tasking,"* which simply meant doing more than one thing at a time. And guess what; this brain dead idiot bought into it.

Multi-tasking means when you're making coffee in the morning, run the water in the pot at the same time you're putting the coffee grounds in the filter. Become multi-productive, why waste that extra 30 seconds of your life, when it could be put to better and more productive use.

Multi-tasking means that when you're driving your son our daughter to practice, be productive by having your cell phone to your ear, while still trying to make your son or daughter think that you are not ignoring them. Not to mention trying to keep your eyes and mind on the road.

We have planned and managed and multi-tasked our schedules to the point that our schedules are now controlling us, instead of us having control over our schedules. While we cannot control time, we can control our schedules and all the events that we try to pack into that time.

In his book, *The Life You've Always Wanted,* John Ortberg[14] cites an article from *Time Magazine* which noted that,

> Back in the 1960's, expert testimony was given to a subcommittee of the Senate on time management. The essence of it was that because of advances in technologies, within twenty years or so people would have to radically cut back on how many hours a week they worked, or how many weeks a year they worked, or else they would have to start retiring sooner. The great challenge they said, was what people would do with all their free time.

Personally I know of very few people who have a lot of free time on their hands. Most retirees will even say they are busier after retirement than before. Why do we do this to ourselves?

Heather Mason, Contributing Editor to the Gallup Organization, reported in a November 2003 article that,

October 24, 2003, was the first annual 'Take Back Your Time Day,' a project of the Center for Religion, Ethics and Social Policy at Cornell University and an initiative of the Simplicity Forum designed to 'challenge the epidemic of overworked, overscheduled and time famine that now threatens our health, our families, our relationships, our communities and our environment.[15]

In December of 1995, Grady McAllister gave a presentation at the University of Houston College of Technology. In his presentation, he cited a quote by Harvard Economics Professor Juliet B. Schor in which she said, "From the end of the 1960's to present, Americans have increased the time spent at work by almost 160 hours—nearly one month—per year."

In addition to a more demanding professional world, during the 80's and 90's we have had an absolute avalanche of organized activities that demanded more and more of our time. These activities are capturing our time, and even more than our time, they are also demanding our mental focus and attention, leaving us with a feeling of being drained, spent, and just down right worn-out. Today we find ourselves going at such a constant pace that we feel at times as if we are in an absolute rat race. It's a race that we're not winning. Even more depressing than the fact that we are in a rat race we're not winning, is the fact that we are fast coming to the realization that there is absolutely no finish line. As noted earlier, Actress

Lily Tomlin once put a little humor into our world of the rat race when she said, "The trouble with a rat race is that even if you win, you're still a rat." That is just what we are beginning to feel like.

But life does not have to be that way. *We* and only *we* are in control of our schedule. While we all complain about how busy our lives have become, I am convinced that we keep up the pace that we do because we feel that if we don't, we will be the loser of the game. We're afraid that we may miss out on something. We fear that if we and our families are not involved in everything all the time, and could not complain about how busy we really are, we will be left behind and thus less important than our peers. Have we evolved to the point that we actually think that if we can't complain about just how busy we are, maybe others will actually think that we live dull, boring, and unproductive lives of little value?

After I retired from business, I tried a little experiment. Whenever someone would ask me if I was busy, I would answer by saying, "Just as busy as I want to be." Almost without exception, the reaction I would get would be a look of almost unbelief that I would even make such a statement. Almost as if it wasn't normal for a person not to be busy, much less admit it.

Not having a hectic rat-racing schedule does not mean one does not have a full and productive life. It just means that life is being managed according to the priorities established. It just means that even as full as life can be, God, not the calendar or the clock, remains the "Objective" of one's life. When we try to be involved in everything, we soon will find that our hearts are in nothing.

Think about your own lifestyle, as well as the lifestyle of your family for a moment. Would you describe your schedule, or that of your family, as sometimes being hectic, chaotic, or even out of control? Would you describe your calendar as being packed to the point of almost being unrealistic? Would you agree that in your pursuit of happiness, you are chasing after the gold ring so hard that it sometimes prohibits you from having a *life* along the way? If you were to agree with any or most of these questions, you shouldn't feel alone, for you're in a very big club. Life for all to many of us has become absolutely packed with a such a hurried and rushed schedule that we often find ourselves unable to enjoy the fruits of our labor, much less enjoy the relationships of family and friends that we cherish the most.

Now I would ask that you compare your life to the life of someone like Mother Teresa. Think about how fruitful and productive her life was. Think about how successful she was in the endeavors she pursued. Think about the positive influence she had on countless others and even the global nature of her ministry. Mother Teresa was a person with whom Heads of State would consider as an absolute honor and privilege just to meet and shake hands with, and yet Mother Teresa is definitely not a person one would associate with having a hectic and chaotic life or lifestyle. One would rather doubt if she ever used a PDA or a laptop computer to keep her on track for what she needed to get done on any given day. One would doubt if she spent any time whatsoever bragging by complaining to others just how busy she was. While the actions of Mother Teresa accomplished a great deal for countless people, and no one could ever argue that Mother Teresa did not have a very full, busy, and productive life, she found her success and her happiness in her *being*, not in her *doing*. Her *doing* came about because of the results of her *being*, not vice-versa, which is often the case for so many of us.

Now I am not suggesting here that we must, or even should, live our lives or have a lifestyle like that of Mother Teresa. For most of us, and our families of today, that would be virtually unrealistic. My point is simply that we can all learn a very valuable lesson from her. Mother Teresa had her priorities in order, and her lifestyle was evidence to it. She accomplished more and was more successful in the endeavors she had pursued than most of us could ever hope for or imagine, yet even with all her success, Mother Teresa never failed to keep God as the "Objective" of her life.

For our life to be productive and successful, it does not mandate the necessity of having a frenzied and constantly hurried lifestyle. Our pursuit of happiness does not have to include that of being a chaotic and continuous rat race against the clock and calendar. If we truly desire, we can have full and complete control of our schedules. To have this complete control simply means that our schedules must truly reflect the priorities that we have established for our lives.

A primary ingredient in putting together our *Life's Strategic Plan* is for us to take control of our lives, and that control must begin with our schedules. Failure to do so will make it very difficult for us to attain the happiness we are in pursuit of, not to mention our ability to keep God as the true "Objective" of our life.

It's Past Our Bedtime

Another area of life that can inhibit us in our pursuit of happiness is in our lack of sleep. An article in *Time Magazine*[16] suggested that Americans have a sleep deficit that is worse than the national budget deficit, and that it results in everything from increased irritability and health problems to fatal car accidents.

Adding credence to that is a Gallup Poll that was conducted in December of 2001. It concluded that 19% of Americans are sleeping five hours or less per night. Another 54% only get between 6 and 7 hours sleep, and only 27% of Americans get a full 8 hours or more. That means that 70% of us are running on less than the optimum of a full 8 hours of sleep. [17]

That compares to a similar survey conducted in 1942 that found that only 3% of Americans were getting fewer than six hours of sleep and 59% were getting eight or more hours of sleep per night. Look at the difference in the lifestyle we are leading today contrasted with that of our parents and grandparents only 40–50 years ago or so. We are definitely becoming a sleep-deprived nation, and it's beginning to take its toll.

According to a study conducted by Dr. Van Cauter, PhD, of the University of Chicago, today we Americans get on an average of 90 minutes less sleep per night than we did in 1960. [18] Think about that for a minute. Statistically speaking, we are getting almost 550 fewer hours of sleep per year than we did in the 60's. Additionally, according to the report cited earlier by Juliet B. Schor, we are working almost 160 hours a year more. That totals 710 hours per year, so is it any wonder that our lives have become a bit chaotic and frazzled.

Realizing of course that not everyone requires a full 8 hours of sleep, yet it is quite safe to say that whatever one's body does require, chances are good that the majority of us are running in this fast-paced, highly stressed out world of ours without ample sleep.

Sleep is a gift to us from God. From Psalm 127 we hear, "It is vain for you to rise early, or put off your rest, You that eat hard-earned bread, for he gives to his beloved in sleep." (Psalm 127:2) God gave us this precious gift of sleep so we could regenerate and rejuvenate our bodies and minds so they could operate at maximum efficiencies. But so often we try to ignore our design and instead take short cuts by depriving ourselves of this precious gift from God. If we would only schedule our lives so we could accept God's gift for the amount of sleep that we need in order to operate at our maximum efficiencies, we would soon discover that our actual accomplishments would increase, our happiness and satisfaction with life would increase, and we would certainly make life better for those who are around us. Additionally, the amount of our stupid mistakes would decrease, and our God would become a greater "Objective" for us in our lives.

We Just Need to Take a Little Break

In addition to amount of sleep we are not getting, we are also depriving ourselves of the much needed basic rest and relaxation. By depriving ourselves of this needed rest and relaxation, we can actually be causing as much, if not more, harm to our families, our careers, and ourselves than we are by not getting ample sleep.

Whereas sleep deprivation makes our bodies tired, worn out and in an unhealthy state, when we deprive ourselves of our needed rest and relaxation, we become mentally and emotionally exhausted. Once we reach that point (many of us are already there), we find it all but impossible to experience happiness with ourselves, our loved ones, our work, and with our God. It is when we are mentally and emotionally exhausted that an attitude of apathy begins to creep in and we lose the passion for the priorities that were once important to us.

While sleep provides our bodies an opportunity to regenerate, rest and relaxation, on the other hand, provide for our mind an opportunity to regenerate. Both are needed if we wish to live a full and productive life. Both are a gift from God, but they are not interchangeable. We need both. Sleep is a matter of *"going down"* for the day. Rest and relaxation is a matter of *"slowing down"* for the day.

The problem of not getting enough rest and relaxation is worse today than it has been at almost anytime throughout the history of our nation. Even with all the time saving devices at our disposal, we find ourselves running till we're ragged from morning to night. While it's true that our entire society is lacking in rest and relaxation, this problem is especially prevalent with young couples that have young, growing and active families, and even more of a problem for the young single parent families. Trying to cram into a 24-hour period all that sometimes needs to get done is becoming more and more of a challenge. Taking into account the normal household chores that can cover the gamut of everything from laundry to cleaning out the gutters and mowing the lawn, and then adding to that all the organized activities of the children plus our professional demands, we soon find not only ourselves, but also the kids running almost out of control from sun up till sun down and beyond, seldom with an opportunity for any breaks. Seldom with any time to just catch our breath.

A good friend of mine was sharing with me

how busy he and his family were. He shared with me of an incident that happened a few nights earlier. He said their typical schedule was that right after school he would drive his son, who was between eight and nine years old at the time, to soccer practice. Then an hour later he would pick him up from practice and drive him to a gymnastic course in which he and his wife had enrolled him. Due to the lateness of the time when gymnastic would be over, they usually stopped at the McDonalds drive-thru to get him a burger to eat on the way. *(Just the type of quality family meal that God had intended!)* He said that one night while driving between the two activities, his young son asked him, "Dad, do I have to go to gymnastic tonight?"

"What would you rather do?" he asked his son.

The answer he got was, "I just wanna go home and ride my bike."

My friend said that he realized at that point that his little boy, who was not even nine years old yet, was on the run from early morning to the time he went to bed, and that even at this young age, he did not have any time to relax and just be a kid. He said upon that realization he made a U-turn toward home and that night he and his wife made the decision that either the gymnastics or the soccer had to go. Kids just need to be kids sometimes.

Not getting ample rest and relaxation sooner or later affects all areas of life, and it especially affects our ability to be good parents. Vince Lombardi once said, "Fatigue makes cowards of us all," and there is no place that this truth becomes more evident than when we're raising our families. When we find our minds and emotions completely "fried" to the point that we are exhausted and worn out, that is when we tend to almost give up and just go with the flow. We have a tendency to just give in to almost every whim of the kids, regardless of their age. Because we are totally exhausted, it's almost out of a feeling of self-survival that sometimes we find it just easier to give into their whims and wants, rather than being the type of parent we really would prefer and know that we should be. Dr. James Dobson said it well with the title of one of his books when he said, *Parenting Isn't for Cowards.* [19] But it is sometimes really hard not to be cowards when fatigue, especially mental fatigue, and total exhaustion have set in to the point that we have lost the energy and the gumption to do what we would otherwise hold as being important.

Our need for more rest and relaxation is an absolute necessity. Even Jesus in his day was well aware of this need. In the sixth chapter of Mark we hear of a time when the demands of life for him and his apostles were getting out of control. When it did, Jesus said to them, "'Come by yourselves to an out-of-the-way place and rest a little.' People were coming and going in great numbers, making it impossible for them to so much as eat. So Jesus and the apostles went off in the boat by themselves to a deserted place." (Mark 6:31–32)

Jesus recognized that they could not keep up their present pace if they intended to be in it for the long run. He decided that it was absolutely necessary for them to leave the crowd behind, at least for a time, and all get away from everyone and everything for their much needed rest and relaxation.

What a great lesson we can get from this one teaching of his. This was the Jesus who could walk on water. Even the one who could make the blind see and the lame walk. Even he needed ample time for rest and relaxation. What gives us the idea that we can go so hard, day in and day out, with such intensity as we sometimes do? Maybe it's time for us to seriously take a hard look at some of the priorities of our lives. Maybe it's about time for us to put together not only *Life's Strategic Plan*, but even more important a manageable plan.

"As We Forgive Those Who Trespass Against Us"

Another critical area in our pursuit of our happiness lies in the area of our ability and willingness to forgive. Most all of us have someone in our lives who, in our opinion, has hurt us considerably. This is someone who has caused a certain degree of pain and suffering by what they have either said or done. This is a person that we find very difficult to grant forgiveness to.

In the vast majority of situations, those who we find hardest to forgive are *not* those who have caused us physical or financial pain or loss, but rather someone who has hurt us emotionally. It's a spouse who has broken a solemn trust. It's an ex-spouse who is using the emotions of the children to get even. It's a parent who abandoned us, a child who is too busy to visit, an ex-partner who took advantage, a friend who turned their back and betrayed us, and the list goes on and on.

Most of us carry the emotional scars left by someone whom we were very close to emotionally, and that has in some way or another, and to one degree or another, harmed us emotionally to the point that we are finding it very difficult to forgive them.

It has been said many times that the line between love and hate is a very thin thread. How often have you witnessed a married couple madly in love one day, and only what seems a short time later are in a heated divorce battle, a battle in which the interest lies more in revenge and causing pain to each other than any of the real issues they may be fighting over.

Or close friends who were at one time almost inseparable, and yet today are not even speaking to each other. The only time the person's name is ever even mentioned is when there is good juicy gossip that can be spread about them.

Or folks who were once close business associates who are now fierce competitors and vicious enemies. Always looking for a way to get the upper hand, with the ultimate goal of either putting each other out of business or causing as much financial harm as possible, and the more the hurt we can cause, the better we *think* we will feel.

While we may attribute our anger and pain to

some physical or financial harm, in reality, however, the pain, anger, and hurt we experience that is by far the more difficult to deal with is the pain and anger that is inflicted as the result of the emotional betrayal that we experience.

If you were to honestly reflect on almost any situation where you have found it difficult to forgive, chances are the offense was due to an emotional betrayal or harm of some sort. It is by far much easier to forgive a physical or financial injury that it is to forgive an emotional hurt or betrayal.

Our inability or unwillingness to forgive some-one who has offended us emotionally causes more pain, agony, stress, sleepless nights, financial losses, and ruined relationships than any other single fac-tor in our lives. Our inability or unwillingness to for-give someone who has offended us emotionally can sometimes be the single most important ingredient in determining the degree of our happiness in this life.

In the worst situations, we find people who become absolutely obsessed with an emotional hurt caused by someone else. They often find their entire mental and emotional energies consumed by the agony of their hurt. A hurt they will not permit to heal. A hurt that may utimately go even so far as to define who they are as a person.

This is someone who is unable to ever enter into a new or lasting relationship because of the emo-tional scars of a previous relationship—scars so deep that they are never permitted to heal, thus the person is prevented from ever going on with life.

These are children and parents who live a life without a loving relationship due to the scars created by one party or the other—scars that continue to fester, because again, they are not permitted to heal.

These are the careers that are lost or become stagnant because of an emotional betrayal and hurt caused by an associate, employer, employee, or business partner, and it is far easier to assess blame than to forgive and allow the hurt to heal and then go on with life.

Evangelist Dr. Robert Schuller once said, "It's not what happens to me that matters most; it's how I react to what happens to me." We live in a world that can sometimes be painful. That is just a fact. Sometimes in this sinful world, we do cause each other pain, hurt and agony. It's never wanted, many times not justified or even fair; many times it is not even intended, but it happens. When it does happen, it's important that we remember that how we react to our injury will have a far more lasting affect than the actual harm or hurt that was created. We may not always have control over the hurt someone may inflict upon us, but we do have total control over how we react to it.

Throughout the scriptures, God has told us over and over again of our need to forgive each other. His desire for us to forgive each other is so important that Jesus told us in the Gospel of Mark:

> Put your trust in God: I solemnly assure you, whoever says to this mountain,

'Be lifted up and thrown into the sea,' and has no inner doubts but believes that what he says will happen, shall have it done for him. I give you my word, if you are ready to believe that you will receive whatever you ask for in prayer, it shall be done for you. *When you stand to pray, forgive anyone against whom you have a grievance* so that your heavenly Father may in turn forgive you your faults. [emphasis added] (Mk 11:22–25)

Jesus is telling us that a prerequisite to even having our prayers being answered is that we need to first forgive anyone who may have hurt us in any way. Our willingness to grant forgiveness to each other is vital to our relationship with our God. He knows that our happiness on this earth will be stifled and hindered until we can first find forgiveness for each other in our hearts. He knows that there is absolutely no way that we could possibly keep him as the true "Objective" of our lives when we are holding a grudge against one of our own brothers or sisters.

But granting forgiveness to someone who has hurt us is never easy. The deeper the hurt, the more we want to hold on to that grudge. Sometimes we have the attitude that by forgiving someone we are in essence saying, "It's okay that you have hurt me, it really doesn't bother me in the least." Which, of course, we know is absolutely not true. Still other times we carry the thought that we may some day, somewhere, somehow make the person pay for their mistake or actions against us, and if we can just get even, then and only then will we feel better. Then and only then will we forgive them.

However, the real basic down-to-earth fact is, whether we grant the person forgiveness or not, as a general rule it will have little or no negative impact on *their* life. Failure on your part to grant forgiveness will adversely affect *your* life ten times greater than it will ever affect the person who may have hurt you.

Whenever we hold a grudge by not forgiving someone, every time we recall the incident of the hurt, our blood begins to boil, our nerves and muscles tighten, and the pain once again quickly comes to the surface. Until we forgive, the hurt will continually resurface, causing us additional pain and anguish. Only by granting true forgiveness from our heart can we put the incident behind us and go on with life once and forever. Martin Luther King, Jr., once said, "Forgiveness is not an occasional act, it is a permanent attitude." When we say we forgive someone, we need to mean it. We need to forgive and then put the pain of the incident behind us.

The granting of forgiveness is far more for the benefit of the *offended* than it is for the *offender*. It is for this very reason that we hear in the Gospel of Matthew the answer Jesus gave to Peter on this very topic when he asked, "'Lord, when my brother wrongs me, how often must I forgive him? Seven times?' 'No,' Jesus said, 'not seven times; I say, seventy times seven times.'" (Matthew 18:21–22) Jesus' point was not that we should be a glutton for punishment and continue to let others hurt us. Rather, his point was that we cannot be free from the pain and anguish of any hurt until we first forgive. As often as others hurt us, that is how often we need to forgive, regardless of the number of times. Because forgiveness is primarily for our own personal benefit, this is the one instance when doing something for ourselves can help and be of benefit. St. Francis of Assisi said, "It is in pardoning that we are pardoned." And it is when we set others free through forgiveness that we are also set free.

Only when we can get rid of all the excess baggage of grudges, bitterness, and feelings of resentment that we may be holding against someone for past hurts and disappointments can we begin to have a clean and fresh slate in our lives. Only then can we keep our God as the "Objective" of our lives. With that clean and fresh slate, we are another step closer to putting together our *Life's Strategic Plan.*

The Stress of Everyday Life
In the Random House College Dictionary, 'stress' is defined as a "physical, mental or emotional tension or strain. While some stress in life is good and needed, today we find that the amount of stress in our lives has increased to the point that it is having a drastically adverse affect on our health, our jobs, and our relationships with God and others.

With all the demands of modern day living, stress in our lives has become a problem of epidemic proportions. Stress in today's society has been called

"Public Enemy Number One." In his book *Coping with the 80's*, Joel Wells says, "Stress is the affliction of the twentieth century."[20] Likewise, *Time Magazine*'s June 6th, 1983, cover story entitled *Stress: Can We Cope* called stress "The Epidemic of the Eighties," and referred to it as our leading health problem in America.[21]

Survey after survey indicates that Americans are under more stress today than that of even a decade or two ago. In 1996, a survey in *Prevention* magazine found that almost 75% feel they have "great stress" at least one day a week, while one out of three felt this way more than twice a week. In the same survey conducted in 1983, only 55% said they felt under great stress on a weekly basis.[22] It has been estimated by some professionals that today 75–90% of all visits to primary care physicians are for stress related problems, and job stress is by far the leading source of stress.

The National Institute for Occupational Safety and Health stated in their publication #99–101, "The nature of work is changing at whirlwind speed. Perhaps now more than ever before, job stress poses a threat to the health of workers, and in turn, to the health organizations."[23] In addition, they cite a survey conducted by Northwestern National Life stating that over 40% of workers report that their job is "extremely stressful."[24] They also site a survey conducted by The Family and Work Institute stating that 26% of workers report that they are "burned out" by the degree of stress in their work.[25]

Some experts approximate that an estimated 1 million workers are absent every day due to stress. The European Agency for Safety and Health at Work reported that over half of the 550 million working days lost annually in the U.S. from absenteeism are stress related. [26]

Experts report emphatically that job stress also exacts a very costly price for U.S. industries and is estimated at over $300 *billion* per year as a result of accidents, absenteeism, employee turnover, diminished productivity, and direct medical, legal and insurance cost, not to mention the cost of workers' compensation awards.

In his book *The Crises of Hope*, Edward Wojciscki says that, "While stress in itself is not an illness, it is a frequent contributor to our emotional and physical distress." He further states that, "while a certain amount of stress in one's life can be a positive force and stimulate us to think more clearly, act more boldly and perform more powerfully, it is clear from the evidence that in all too many cases stress gets the best of us. It overwhelms, and burns us out." [27]

Often interpretations of stress at the workplace is confused and wrongly labeled as one's job or work simply being "challenging." A "challenge," on one hand, will energize us psychologically and physically, and it will further motivate us to learn new skills and master new jobs. When a challenge is met, we feel relaxed and satisfied. Thus a challenge is an important ingredient for healthy and productive work.

Stress, on the other hand, is present when the

challenge has turned into demands that cannot be met, relaxation has turned to exhaustion, and a sense of satisfaction has turned into a feeling of frustration and burn-out, setting the stage for illness, injury, and job failure.

So far we have only scratched the surface as to the devastating effect that stress is having in our society, for we have only discussed stress in the workplace. But stress in our personal and family life is equally as prominent. There are several factors that are the culprits contributing to our stress.

To begin, we need to consider the fact that by far the majority of both husbands and wives work outside the home. According to Harvard Economics Professor Juliet Schor, "Americans work more hours than any other industrial country except Japan." However, she also noted that that difference between our two countries is offset by the fact that Japan has a mostly male workforce. [28] We in America are just the opposite. So now instead of having just one spouse bringing their work and their high degree of stress home with them, we have two. Two people coming home after eight, ten, or more hours of having their nerves and stress levels stretched almost to the point of breaking. It would be great if when the couple came home they could relax together and enjoy a nice glass of wine and have a relaxing candle-lit dinner with soft music. But that is far from reality for the majority. For most of us, we have yet a long way to go and a lot to do before our heads ever hit the pillow. In addition to all the normal household chores of laundry, dishes, yard work, and home maintenance, we also have bills to pay, kids' homework to contend and assist with, kids' sporting events and practices to attend (or at least be the taxi to and from), as well as committee and/or church meetings and projects of our own to complete, and all that is on a relatively slow week.

That's the typical daily agenda for the married couple. Consider just how much more hectic it is for the single parent who is attempting to hold down a stress-filled job and also hold the family together all at the same time, all by one's self, yet still having many of the same items on their plate as their friends who are married.

Then add to that all the stress that often enters into one's life as a result of some of life's everyday occurrences, such as worries over finances, illness, job stability, retirement concerns, concerns over college costs, death of loved ones, job transfers, divorce or separations, and a host of other factors that are some of the stressors of everyday life.

Then we need to consider the degree of stress that our kids are experiencing in our world today, as confirmed by many of the same reports and surveys. Seldom are our children permitted to come home after school and simply be kids. In addition to their normal homework, they also have schedules that are almost a match to our own.

When considering the full scope of our lives and the lives of our families, is it any wonder that romance has gone out of a lot of marriages? Is it any wonder we have lost the ability to communicate? Is it any wonder so many of our kids are now on prescription medication for hypertension and A.D.H.D.?

When we are all experiencing the level of stress in our lives that we are, it is all but impossible for us to have the quality of life that we had hoped this great society of ours was going to provide. The more stress we experience, the more of a need we have for instant gratification. As mentioned previously, instant gratification is not only very temporary in nature, but also often fruitless in providing the actual satisfaction and fulfillment we are both searching for and in need of.

To expect to live a life in today's world, however, without any stress is not realistic. As Stanford psychiatrist David Spiegel put it, "Living a stress-free life is not a reasonable goal. The goal is to deal with it actively and effectively." [29]

According the National Mental Health Association, "Stress often creates its largest problems when we lose control of it in our lives." [30] It is when our bodies and minds are constantly reacting to stressful situations without our making adjustments to counter the effects that the stress begins to threaten our health and well-being, not to mention the adverse affect it has on the quality of our family life, the relationship we have with friends, and our relationship with our God. When stress takes control of our lives, our main and primary focus tends to be on self-survival. That is when we begin to manage our lives by "crises" rather than by "objective."

To counter not only the adverse affects that

stress can cause in your life, but in addition, in an attempt to reduce your stress, the National Mental Health Association offers the following suggestions:[31]

- **Be Realistic**: Determine *your* tolerance level for stress and try to live within these limits. If you feel overwhelmed, learn to say no. Eliminate an activity that is not absolutely necessary.

- **Shed the superman/superwoman urge**: No one is perfect; so don't expect perfection from yourself or others. Ask yourself what is really realistic. What adjustments can be made to your schedules or current workload? Don't hesitate to ask for help if needed.

- **Meditate**: Just ten to twenty minutes of quiet reflection may bring relief from chronic stress as well as increase your tolerance for it. *(More on this in the next chapter)*.

- **Visualize**: Use your imagination and picture how you can manage a stressful situation more successfully. Whether it's a business presentation or moving to a new place, many people find visual rehearsals boost self-confidence and enable them to take a more positive approach to a difficult task.

- **Take one Thing at a Time**: For people under tension or stress, an ordinary workload can sometimes seem unbearable. The best way to cope with this feeling of being overwhelmed is to take one task at a time. Pick one urgent task and work on it. The positive feeling of "checking off" tasks is very satisfying. It motivates one to keep on going.

- **Exercise**: Regular exercise is a popular and effective way to relieve stress. Twenty to thirty minutes of physical activities benefit both body and mind. Studies have shown that stress causes hormones such as adrenaline to be released into the body, and exercise is a perfect way to release that adrenaline.

- **Hobbies**: Take a break from your worries and stress by doing something you enjoy. Whether it's gardening, painting, fishing, golfing, or a leisure bike ride, schedule time to indulge your interest.

- **Healthy lifestyle**: Good nutrition makes a difference. Limit intake of caffeine and alcohol. Get adequate rest and sleep as discussed previously. Most of all, balance work and its priorities with the rest of your life.

- **Share your feelings**: A conversation with a spouse, a special friend or loved one, gives the reassurance that you're not in this game alone. You're not the only one who is having a bad day or experience problems, stress or worries. Keeping it as pent-up frustrations and worry only magnifies the problem. If all else fails, seek out a health professional or your clergy to speak to. Don't try to cope alone.

- **Give in occasionally. Be flexible!** If you find you're meeting constant opposition in either your personal or professional life, rethink your position or strategy. Arguing only intensifies stressful feelings. If you know you are right, stand your ground, but do so calmly and rationally. Make allowances for others' opinions and be prepared to compromise. If you are willing to give in, others may meet you half-way. Not only will you reduce your stress, you may find better solutions to your problems.

One final suggestion when it comes to stress in life: try to find that fine line between the times when we take life far too seriously, and those times that we do not take it serious enough.

When we do not take life seriously enough, we often find ourselves trying to play catch-up or reworking something because we failed to take it seriously enough the first time around. This also creates additional stress in our lives.

On the other hand, when we take life too seriously is when we fail to live a life along the way. As Albert Einstein once said, "Once you can accept the universe as matter expanding into nothing, that is in itself something, wearing stripes with plaid comes very easy." Most of us get far too stressed out over the stripes and plaids of life.

Problems of Everyday Life

Life is a series of problems, and needless to say, our problems will have a great affect on our happiness. As a general rule, as soon as we solve one problem, there is another to take its place. Some of our problems are quite small in nature, almost to the point of being nothing more than a simple irritant. Irritants like that of the paperboy throwing the paper on the lawn instead of on the front porch. Or maybe it's when the sacker at the grocery store puts the gallon of milk in the same bag as the bread. Nonetheless, depending on what else in going on in our lives at the time, we may react to those little irritants as if they are major issues.

Other problems are more in the nature of what might be considered as just another typical problem we need to deal with in life. Maybe it's a problem at work with a co-worker that keeps rearing its ugly head and seems never to be resolved. Or maybe it a mechanical problem with the car that is going to cost more to repair than our current budget can handle. Or maybe one of your teenage kids was in a minor fender-bender accident and due to their inexperience or negligence, or a little of both, they were charged with failure to have their car under control, and you just know that your insurance rates are going to go through the roof.

Then there are the problems in life that are considered major. A serious health problem of a loved one or yourself that is keeping you awake at night in worry and wonder of what the future may bring. Or a problem in an intimate relationship that you are unsure can or will ever be reconciled.

Problems are an inherent part of our lives and the condition of our human nature that resulted from the fall of Adam and Eve. As long as we are here on this earth and not experiencing the joys of God's Kingdom in Heaven, we will have and experience problems. As I said earlier, whenever we solve one problem, another is right there to take its place. Unfortunately, many times the problem that replaces the previous problem is one that we created ourselves by the very solution of the problem we wanted to resolve.

For example: We have a problem that the car

is beyond repair, so we trade it off for a new one, one for which we now have higher payments, and that creates a new problem with the budget. So to resolve that problem we take on extra hours at work, which creates a new problem by our not being able to spend as much time with the family, which creates another problem, and the solution to that can often create another problem, and so life goes.

While we can all thank God that by far the vast majority of our problems of life fall into more of the "everyday" type or even the little "irritant" type, yet we all experience, at one time or another, problems that are very serious in nature. These are problems that, in many cases, are the kind from which we may never totally recover. Problems that are totally outside of our control and not necessarily brought on by anything that we have done or should have done; Problems that can be so devastating that they rock the very foundation of our lives and sometimes even that of our faith. For example, these are the times when we lose a loved one in death due to an unexpected illness or accident. These are the problems that lead us to ask, "Why God? Why me? What did I do wrong that I deserved this?" These are the tragic problems in life to which there is no answer that could ever be sufficient or adequate to satisfy the anguish or pain that we are experiencing. These are the problems such that when we are going through them, we tend to wonder if we will ever be able to smile or laugh again. These are the problems that arise in life that leave us with absolutely no one to whom we can turn for help, except to our God, whom we can look to for just one more ounce of strength to get us through the situation. As Mother Teresa said, "You will never know that Jesus is all you need, until Jesus is all you've got."

When our problems are such that we have nowhere else to turn is when, above all other times, we need to rely on our faith and the assurances of our God that one way or another, we will be able to overcome the problem and see the sun on another day. Maybe not in the way that we had hoped or wanted, but that is where trust in our God, who is God, must come into the picture. In the Book of Isaiah we are given this assurance from God when we hear, "When you pass through the water, I will be with you; in the rivers you shall not drown. When you walk through fire, you shall not be burned; the flames shall not consume you" (Isaiah 43:2), and then in Psalm 50 he tells us, "Then call upon me in times of distress; I will rescue you, and you shall glorify me." (Psalm 50:15a) For our God, who an is all-knowing and all-loving God, reveals to us in the Epistle of Paul to the Romans, "I consider the sufferings of the present to be as nothing compared with the glory to be revealed in us. Indeed, the whole created world eagerly awaits the revelation of the sons of God." (Romans. 8:18–19)

The more we look to our faith to get us through our difficult and serious problems and situations of life, the stronger our faith will become, and the more our God will become the "Objective" of our lives.

Elizabeth Kubler-Ross, who researched extensively and wrote on the five stages of grief, said, "People are like stained-glass windows. They sparkle and shine when the sun is out, but when the darkness sets in, their true beauty is revealed only if there is a light from within." When all other light goes out in our world, it is then that we need to look to our God to keep the light within us glowing.

These major problems definitely have an impact on the degree of happiness we experience in life, especially as we are going through them. But as we stated earlier, we can thank our God that by far the vast majority of the problems we experience in life are not in the category of being serious or catastrophic in nature. For as also stated above, most of our problems fall into the category of the "typical" or "irritating" problems of life, yet believe it or not, many times these problems have far more impact on who we become as a person than the major problems do. The reason for this is simple.

First, the major problems occur very infrequently, and when they do, we usually have the support of family and friends to help us through them. The second reason is due to the personality that we form and the individual we become as a result of the attitude and reaction we have toward our daily problems. Charles Swindoll said, "I am convinced that life is 10% what happens to me and 90% how I react to it." How true that statement is. What happens to us in life is one thing; how we react to it is something altogether different. How we react to all our everyday and little irritating problems of life will have a direct impact on the degree of happiness we experience in this world.

We have all heard the statement that "he (or she) is their own worse enemy." By this statement we often imply that the person creates more problems and unhappiness for themselves than are caused by outside forces. While we like to think that that is the case only for "other people," the fact is, however, that most all of us fall into this category at one time or another. If the truth is admitted, a great many of our problems of this life are caused by our own actions, and/or by the way we react to life's many situations.

This is a fact that is hard for us to admit, because it's always so much easier to blame others or circumstances that are beyond our control than it is to accept responsibility for our own actions.

The more we tend to take the responsibility for our own problems, the more time and consideration we will give to our decisions. The more we accept responsibility for our problems, the easier it will be for us to resolve them and then go on with life.

It is when we place the total blame on others that we expect others to come to our aid to solve our problem. We may be waiting a long time for any resolution to occur if we are looking to the wrong person as the cause of the problem. When we don't take responsibilities for our own problems, we have a tendency to play the "poor me" game. Until we take full responsibility, we will continue to wallow in them and never rise above them. Winston Churchill once said, "If you're going through hell, keep going." If you have a problem, acknowledge it, admit to it, solve it, resolve it, and then get on with life. Wallowing in it will not change anything; it will only make it worse for you, and certainly for those around you.

Worry

Another area that causes us a great deal of unhappiness in life is when we create problems in our own mind or even make our problems worse by worrying about them.

Jesus knew well that worry adversely affected not only our happiness, but also our relationships with both God and others. Numerous places in Scripture instruct us on the topic of worry. In the Gospel of Matthew we are told, "Enough, then, of worrying about tomorrow. Let tomorrow take care of itself. Today has troubles enough of its own" (Matthew 6:34). Jesus also says in Matthew, "I warn you then: do not worry about your livelihood, what you are to eat or drink or use for clothing. Is not life more than food? Is not the body more valuable than clothes? Which of you by worrying can add a moment to his life-span?" (Matthew 6:25, 27)

I once read a statement that said something like, "Your ship is equal to the load of today; but when you are carrying yesterday's worry and tomorrow's anxiety, lighten up, or you will sink."

If only we could do that. Or maybe a better statement is "If only we *would* do that." But even with all the instructions and advice we have received from God as well as our health professionals on the devastating affect that worry can have on our lives and how little value it is in resolving anything, how many of us spend a great deal of time worrying about what *might* happen, or in anxiety for what *could* happen? We find ourselves worrying about everything from the serious to the mundane. Mark Twain once said, "I am an old man and have known a great many troubles, most of them never happened."

I once had a parishioner say to me, "Don't tell me that worry doesn't do any good. I know better. The things I worry about don't happen." You know, sometimes it just does not pay to confuse people with facts.

Worry seldom if ever changes the outcome of things. The only thing worry does is create more stress in our lives and more harm to our health. A sleepless, worry-filled night spent tossing and turning does no good for anyone and seldom does anything to resolve a problem. Dale Carnegie always taught that, "If you can't sleep, then get up and do something instead of lying there worrying. It's the worry that gets you, not the lack of sleep."

Whenever you get tied down with daily problems and concerns, remember the good advice from Ralph Waldo Emerson: "Finish each day and then be done with it. You have done what you could; some blunders and absurdities have crept in; forget them as soon as you can. Tomorrow is a new day; you shall begin it serenely and with too high a spirit to be encumbered with your old nonsense."

Summary

The pursuit of happiness for the vast majority of us is well within our reach. The deciding factor is how we live our lives and the priorities to which we hold ourselves. Each of the factors toward happiness as discussed in this chapter will have either a positive or negative affect on our ability to realize a degree of happiness here on earth. While there is no such thing as absolute or lasting happiness in this life, we can live our lives with a sense of satisfaction, fulfillment, and peace if we hold ourselves true to our values, have our priorities in order, and keep our God as the true "Objective" of our lives. C.S. Lewis once wrote, "God cannot give us happiness and peace apart from himself, because it is not there. There is no such thing." It is when we attempt to go our own way, using only worldly standards and the priorities set by society that we find ourselves in trouble. Our loving God has set the path for us. He has provided the road map and the direction for how to get there. We only need to follow it.

Happy are those who reap the Lord's Reward

Happy are you who fear the Lord,
Who walk in his ways!
For you shall eat the fruits of your handiwork;
Happy shall you be, and favored.
Your wife shall be like a fruitful vine
in the recess of your home;
Your children like olive plants around your table.
Behold, thus is the man blessed who fears the Lord.
The Lord bless you from Zion:
May you see the prosperity of Jeru-
salem all the days of your life;
May you see your children's children.

(Psalm 128:1–6a)

chapter nine

Prayer and Worship

In this, our last chapter before we begin to put together our *Life's Strategic Plan* we will discuss the two very important factors in our plan that will be mandatory if we truly hope to keep our God as the "Objective" of our life. As the title of this chapter suggests, we will be discussing the various aspects of our prayer and worship.

Based on all the polls and surveys taken, most of us indicate that we pray daily. A survey in a *Newsweek* article from January 6th, 1992, entitled *Talking to God: An intimate look at the way we pray* found that more Americans said that they pray in a given week than those who work, exercise, or even have sexual relations. In fact, of the 13% of Americans who claim to be atheist or agnostic, even one in five of them claim to pray daily. [32] This reminds me of the statement of the atheist who once said, "I hope and pray that there is no God, but then when I really think about it, I then just hope there is no God."

Our God has planted himself in the hearts of each and every one of us. In the Book of Ecclesiastes we read, "He has made everything appropriate to its time, and has put the timeless into their hearts, with-

141

out men's ever discovering, from beginning to end, the work which God has done." (Ecclesiastes 3:11) Because we cannot see the whole scope of God's work from beginning to end, that is why he has also gifted us with the inner need and ability for personal prayer. In the Acts of the Apostles we read, "so that people might seek God, even perhaps grope for him and find him, though indeed he is not far from any one of us. For 'Indeed we live and move and have our being,' as even some of your poets have said, 'For we too are his offspring.' (Acts 17:27–28)

The problem that arises, however, is in the meaning and style that determines what prayer is to us. We have become very accustomed to using the term "prayer" to imply a vast variety of our thoughts and feelings.

For the majority of us Americans, we have become very accustomed to what we interpret as the "praying" to God throughout the day in one form or the other. But the real question may be, what exactly do our prayers consist of? When we say the word "pray" or "prayer," what is it we are really meaning? Do we pray with the expectation that our prayers will be heard, and even more important to us, will they be answered? Do we pray out of desire, or do we find ourselves praying most often when we feel it is only our last resort?

Prayer for each of us can mean many different things, and the reason why it is different is because we each have a unique and different relationship with our God. Prayer and worship, then, are about relationship. In this chapter we will discuss the various factors that can aid us in developing and nurturing a quality and intimate relationship with our God.

Personal & Private Prayer

As human beings, we develop all our relationships in a very similar fashion. For any relationship to flourish and grow it has to be a two way street. Consider what a relationship would be like with anyone whom we desired an intimate relationship with if the main interactions would consist only of times when we would be asking of them to either "Please give to me" or "Please help me." Any relationship built in such a fashion is, at best, built on very sandy soil. Jesus himself referred to such a shallow relationship when he said:

> Why do you call me Lord, Lord and not put into practice what I teach you? Any man who desires to come to me will hear my words and put them into practice. I will show you with whom he is to be compared. He may be likened to the man who in building a house, dug deeply and laid the foundation on a rock. When the floods came the torrents rushed in on that house, but failed to shake it because of its solid foundation. On the other hand, anyone who has heard my words but not put them into practice is like the man who built his house on the ground without any foundation. When the torrent

rushed upon it, it immediately fell in and
was completely destroyed. (Luke 6:46–49)

Any relationship that is shallow and built on
sand will soon find itself going sour at the first sign
of the slightest interruption. By its very definition,
for a relationship to be intimate, both parties must be
committed to it. For a relationship to become solid
and intimate, it takes time, it takes a commitment,
and most important of all, it takes a sincere desire.

Unfortunately for many of us, our daily personal prayer is too often limited to the *"Lord Grant
Me"* or the *"Lord Help Me"* type of prayer. While
it is true that Jesus told us that we should take *"all
things"* to him in prayer, how seldom is it that we
spend quality time in prayer for the sole purpose of
developing a quality, intimate relationship with our
God. Seldom are we committed to the desire of actually building a relationship with Him through our
prayers.

Archbishop Fulton Sheen once said this about
prayer:

Prayer is not just informing God of our
needs, for he already knows them. God does
not show himself equally to all creatures.
This does not mean that he has favorites,
that he decides to help some and to abandon
others, but the difference occurs because it
is impossible for him to manifest himself to
certain hearts under the conditions they set
up. The sunlight plays no favorites, but its

reflection is very different on a lake than on a swamp.

When we think or feel that our prayers are mere empty words and thoughts, maybe the first place we need to look is at the relationship we have with our God. It's always much easier to have an intimate conversation with a loving spouse or a good friend than it is with someone with whom we have only a casual acquaintance. Prayer is about relationship. The better our relationship, the more meaningful our prayer becomes. The more meaningful our prayer life, the more important prayer becomes to us. The more important it becomes, the easier we find it to pray. The easier we find it to pray, the better and more intimate our relationship with our God becomes. It all works hand in hand. And as Archbishop Sheen said, "The sun reflects different on a lake than it does on a swamp."

In the book *The Life You've Always Wanted,* John Ortberg put this slant on personal prayer when he said, "In addition to all the other work that gets done through prayer, perhaps the greatest work of all is the knitting of the human heart together with the heart of God." [33] Whenever hearts are knitted together, that is when an intimate and solid relationship develops, a relationship that can and will withstand the most trying of circumstances or events of our lives.

Of course, Jesus had that special intimate relationship with his Father in Heaven. Time after time throughout the Scripture, Jesus taught by his example of the need to set aside that special time for prayer and the building of that intimate relationship with God. In Matthew 14, we read that, "When he had sent them away, he went up on the mountain by him self to pray." (Matthew 14:23) Then Jesus gives us yet another lesson when we hear, "Then he went out to the mountain to pray, spending the night in communion with God." (Luke 6:12) Also in the ninth chapter of Luke we hear that, "he took Peter, John and James, and went up the mountain to pray." (Luke 9:28b) For Jesus, prayer was a very important and vital ingredient in his everyday life. While it can be said that without a doubt, as the only begotten son of God, Jesus' entire life was a constant prayer to the Father, yet even he found the need and the wisdom for setting aside that special time each day for prayer.

But who has time for that? When we're already going from morning till night and at times find it difficult to even sit down together as a family for an evening meal, how can we fit time for private prayer into our already full schedule? Doesn't God understand? Isn't he with me and doesn't he hear me just as much when I pray to him in my car or on the subway as I'm on my way to work as he does when I am on my knees beside my bed?

Of course the answer to all those questions is without any doubt a resounding *yes*. Yes, he understands that your life is busy and sometimes very hectic. Yes, he is with you and hears you just as much when you pray in the car or on the subway as when you are on your knees beside your bed. But remember, prayer is about a relationship. True, intimate relationships are built when both time and attention are devoted to it.

Time is a very precious gift with which God has blessed each of us. Yet it is that very gift of time that is the single largest obstacle that we need to overcome before we can have the positive and quality prayer life and develop the relationship with our God that he desires and our souls long after. It's not so much that we don't have time, rather it's because we don't take the time. It's been said that you must never *"find"* time for anything. If you want time you must *"take it."*

Regardless of our schedule in life, the more busy, hectic, and chaotic it becomes the more of a need we have for a quality prayer life. When Martin Luther found his life hectic and sometimes out of control he would say, "I am so busy now that if I did not spend two or three hours each day in prayer, I would not get through the day." In the same vein, Saint Francis of Sales wrote, "Every Christian needs a half hour of prayer each day, except when they're busy, then they need an hour." And St. Francis of Assisi said, "I am so busy today that I will need to spend another hour in prayer."

Prayer becomes most important to us when life becomes busy, hectic, and sometimes out of control. It is when life becomes that way that above all times we need the solid relationship with our God and Savior. That is when we need prayer and our relationship with our God the most.

Bottom line: if you desire a personal and intimate relationship with God, then personal prayer on a regular and routine bases is the first prerequisite. Personal prayer not only puts God as the "Objective" of your life, it also keeps him there through the relationship that we both build and maintain with him.

Solitude

I have a good friend who works for a major Corporation. The job he has, like that of many today, is somewhat stressful. In a discussion one day he was explaining to me about a few policies his company had in place for the welfare of the employees.

As he explained them, these polices were divided into three categories. The first category was vacation time. He said that every employee after two years of employment was not only entitled, but also required to take 3 weeks of annual vacation. A requirement of the vacation time was that employees were permitted to take only one of those three weeks on a day here & day there basis. For the remaining two weeks however, their policy dictated that employees must take a minimum of a full week away from the office. The rationale of the policy was that the company felt that employees could not adequately regenerate both body and mind by taking only an occasional day away from the office.

The second category came in the area of hobbies. It was the policy of the company that every employee must have a hobby that they could be almost passionate toward. If their hobby was seasonal like that of playing golf, for example, then they needed more than one. The company knew well the benefit of quality recreation in the life of their employees.

The third category came in the area of community service. Now while the community definitely benefited from the service of their employees, that was only the byproduct of the policy. The true reason for this policy was that the company wanted their employees to have a committed interest outside of both work and recreation.

My friend reported that the result of these three simple polices for this company was that they suffered less turnover and burnout, less absenteeism, and fewer complaints among their workers than before they implemented the polices.

The need to get away from things for a period of time was also a need for Jesus. Scriptures tell us that following his baptism in the Jordan by John, "Jesus was led into the desert by the Spirit . . . He fasted forty days and forty nights . . ." (Matthew 4:1a-2a) Jesus left everyone and everything behind so he could take the time to focus on who he was, and what his life was all about. He took this time to solidify his relationship with his God and become one with his Father in Heaven.

In addition to the extended periods, Jesus also escaped from the pressures of life numerous times for shorter periods. For example, following the death of John the Baptist, we hear in the Gospel of Matthew that "When Jesus heard this, he withdrew by boat from there to a deserted place by himself." (Matthew 14:13a) Again, after Jesus preached to and fed the crowd of five thousand we hear that "Immediately afterward, while dismissing the crowds, Jesus insisted that his disciples get into the boat and preceded him to the other side. When he had sent them away, he went on the mountain by himself to pray, remaining there alone as evening drew on." (Matthew 14:22–24a)

The need to get away for a period of solitude as a time for reflection and coming together as one with our God has never been greater than it is for us today, with our busy and sometimes hectic and chaotic schedules. Thomas Edison once said that, "The best thinking has been done in solitude. The worst has been done in turmoil." But ask yourself, when you need to do your best thinking, as a general rule where do you find yourself, in solitude or in turmoil?

In an earlier chapter we had discussed the need for sleep, rest, and relaxation to regenerate and rejuvenate our minds and bodies. In this segment we will briefly discuss the need for solitude to regenerate and rejuvenate our spiritual well-being.

Fr. Henri Nouwen said, "Solitude is the furnace of transformation." That's the sole purpose for solitude, it's a time for transformation. While time of solitude is not a vacation, it is a respite from everyday life. Time spent in solitude is not necessarily a time for long periods of rigorous and formal prayer from our minds, rather an intentional and continuous prayer from our heart and a time of transformation of the soul for communication and communion with God.

Fr. Nouwen further says that:

> Our primary task in solitude is . . . to keep the eyes of our mind and heart on him who is our divine Savior . . . only with a single-minded attention to Christ can we give up our clinging fears and face our own true nature. As we come to realize that it is not we who live, but Christ who lives in us, that he is our true self, we can slowly let our compulsions melt away and begin to experience the freedom of the children of God . . .
>
> In solitude, our heart can slowly take off its many protective devices and can grow so wide and deep that nothing human is strange to it . . .
>
> It's then that we can give birth to a new awareness reaching far beyond the boundaries of our human efforts. And then we, who in our fearful narrow-mindedness, were afraid that we would not have enough food for ourselves, will have to smile.

Solitude helps us bring everything into perspective, and gives our soul a time to catch its breath.

Solitude, in the context that I am defining it here, is *one being alone with or just wasting time with God.* It's not a time for learning or education, nor a time for personal recreation. It is also not time to be spent with spouse, kids, or friends. While all of these can bring God closer to us in our lives, nonetheless they are not times of solitude.

Solitude is time that we spend *alone* with our God for the specific and intent purpose of getting in touch with and communicating with Him. Solitude is not a time that we spend worrying about our problems, cares, and concerns, but rather a time that we turn all of our problems, cares, and concerns over to our God. It's a time when we finally quit talking and begin to listen. Archbishop Fulton Sheen once said that, "Prayer begins by talking to God, but it ends by listening to him. In the face of Absolute Truth, silence is the soul's language." Solitude is where we find that silence and the language of the soul that is able to listen to our God in the midst of our world today.

Just as our minds and bodies cannot unwind and regenerate themselves by only taking a day here and day there away from the normal routine of life, so, too, it is with our souls. In this fast-paced, sometimes very hectic and chaotic commercialized world we live in, it's easy for us to fall in to the rut that ever so gradually can pull us away from our God. Life has a tendency to pull us ever so gradually and ever so easily into a rut so that after a while, God is no longer the "Objective" of our life. Rather, life itself, with all its stress, challenges, and personal desires becomes our primary, if not only, focus.

In the ideal situation, we would be able to take extended periods of time that we could devote to and be in solitude with our God. By extended periods of time, I am suggesting a full 24 hours as a minimum, and even two or more days if at all possible. For extended periods of solitude, it is by far best to get away to a retreat center where someone can assist you with suggestions for you to get maximum benefit from your time of solitude. If you are unaware of retreat centers in your local area, check with your pastor or local clergy. By far, the majority of clergy that I know make an annual retreat themselves for this very purpose. For me, my retreat time is not only a very important time for me, but in many ways it is also a vital time for me to regroup and put my life back in to real perspective. In the past 20 years or so, I think there were only two years that I was unable to go on a retreat I had already scheduled due to family commitments and obligations that had to take priority. It really does become a matter of both scheduling and prioritizing. For me, my retreat and time of solitude with my God has become a valued priority in my life.

But extended periods of two or more days may not be a reality or even possible for many who already have very busy lives, at least at this point in their lives. One of my young daughters-in-law once told me that the closest thing she can get to periods of solitude is when she can be in the bathroom for a few minutes alone, without one of the little ones coming in, the phone ringing, or someone yelling *"Mom!"* However, it is just for such a mom that quality time spent in solitude is so *desperately needed.*

If two or more days, or even a full 24 hours is not possible, try spending the 8 hours or so that you would normally spend at work. Take a personal day off from work and still take the kids to the sitter or day care, but instead of going to work, spend it as a day of reflection and solitude with your God. Go to a religious bookstore or ask your pastor to recommend a good book for reflection. If at all possible, get away from home and all its familiar surroundings. Go to a park or another area where you can be close to nature and the beauty of God's creation. Spend the day doing some reading, but don't spend the entire day reading. Spend time in prayer, but don't spend the entire day in formal or focused prayer. Most importantly, spend time focusing on your relationship with your God. And above all, spend time listening to and becoming one with God. This is your day with God, so use it wisely and don't let anyone rob you of it. Get away to be by yourself at a place where there can be quite and solitude, and be sure you shut your cell phone off.

If it's not possible or feasible to get out of the house for your day of solitude, then spend it at home, but spend the day in the same way. Be sure you unplug the TV, radio, and again, shut off the cell phone and put the phone in the house on silent. This is your day with God. It's not a day to do the shopping, clean the house, do the laundry, or mow the lawn. It's because of the possible temptation of doing some of the needed chores around the house that it's always best to get away if at all possible. This is your day with God, and is a day for you to focus on your *"being,"* not on *"doing."*

This day must be planned or it will never happen. Husbands and wives should work together to assure that each is able to have their own one full day or more of solitude each year. You will discover that the benefits of your days of solitude will far exceed what one would imagine.

In addition to your annual day or days of solitude, one should also practice shorter periods of solitude throughout the year. These are the periods throughout the week that we find that we are alone for maybe an hour or so and can take advantage of it and spend it as solitude time with our God.

Perhaps these are times when we are traveling alone and we turn off the radio or CD and place ourselves in his presence. I had a friend of mine say that her travel time to work is about 45 minutes. She told me that a minimum of twice a week she turns off the radio and spends that time in solitude with her God.

Perhaps these are times when we find ourselves at home alone and we turn off the TV, radio, and put the newspaper down and just relax for an hour or so, placing our minds and hearts in the comfort of God's presence.

Perhaps these are the times when we are able to go for that long walk along the nature trail, and instead of having a headset on listening to our favorite music, we instead focus our mind on a leisurely stroll in talking *and listening* to our God.

Perhaps these are the times when we go for a bike ride and without any goal of either destination or speed, we instead concentrate on our relationship with and listening to God.

Perhaps these are the times when we can lie out under the stars on a warm summer night and concentrate on the wonders of God's creation and on how even in the vastness of all the universe we can marvel at the very thought of how precious and personal we are to him.

I think that gives you the idea. Most all of us, whether at home, work, or even traveling, have many opportunities to spend time in solitude with our God. Solitude is a matter of bringing our gifts, our gratitude, our problems, our worries, our entire life, and everything that we are into the presence of God, and then simply being quiet and listening. The more that is on our plate of life that we bring to him, the more time we may need to listen.

Begin the practice of solitude with a commitment of an hour or so several times a month, and then schedule that personal day when you can spend the entire day in solitude with your God. The more time you spend in solitude with him just listening, the more valuable you will find it, and the closer you will grow to him. By listening to him more often, He will truly become the true "Objective" of your life.

Worship

The term "worship" means many different things to different people. The secular *Random House College Dictionary* defines it as "reverent honor and homage paid to God or a sacred personage, or any object regarded as sacred."

The *International Standard Bible Encyclopedia* states that in the Old Testament, the word "worship" is derived from a word that means to *Bow Down* or to *Prostrate.* Some of the Aramaic words of the Old Testament indicate that "to worship is to render service." Therefore, as they state it, "the Old Testament idea of worship is the reverential attitude of mind or body or both with the more generic notion of religions adoration, obedience, and service." [34]

The same encyclopedia also states that in the New Testament, the term "worship" is primarily associated with one's attitude of "rendering homage." It states that 59 times, the New Testament refers to worship in the sense of "to kiss the hand or the ground" or "bowing in prostrate." Therefore, in the New Testament the term "worship" is primarily attributed to "reverence" or, even more profoundly, to the "holding in awe."

So to give God the worship that he is due, we humbly lay our entire lives before him. It is through the gift of life, and what we do with that life, that we worship him through our obedience, our service, our reverence, and our prayers, all resulting in our profoundly holding him in awe. It is in everything that we do, say, think, and are that we give continued praise, honor, and glory to our God, because He is God.

In Psalm 100 we hear the psalmist giving worship and glory to God as he prays,

> Sing joyfully to the Lord, all you lands; serve the Lord with gladness; come before him with joyful song. Know that the Lord is God, he made us, his we are; his people, the flock he tends. Enter his gates with thanksgiving, his courts with praise; Give thanks to him; bless his name, for he is good: The Lord, whose kindness endures forever, and his faithfulness, to all generations. (Psalm 100:1–5)

Our desire and need to give him praise, honor and glory is an inborn gift with which He has blessed each one of us. In the prayer of the Fourth Weekday Preface for the Catholic Mass we hear,

> Father, all powerful and ever-living God, we do well always and everywhere to give you thanks. You have no need for our praise, yet our desire to thank you is itself your gift. Our prayer of thanksgiving adds nothing to your greatness, but makes us grow in your grace through Jesus Christ our Lord. In our joy we sing to your glory with all the choirs of angels.

As this prayer so appropriately indicates, our need and desire to give our God the praise and honor that he is due adds nothing to his greatness, but even our desire to praise him is in itself a treasured gift from God. St. Thomas Aquinas said, "We pay God honor and reverence, not for his sake (because he is of himself full of glory to which no creature can add anything), but for our own sake."

But as with any gift, we can use or misuse it. God has given us the freedom to make our own decision as to whether we will use or lose the gift of our desire to praise him.

It is true that we do indeed give praise, honor and glory to His Holy Name in all and everything that we do through our service, actions, and attitudes of our daily life. However, we most fittingly and most appropriately give to him the true reverence that he is due, and most profoundly hold him in awe when we worship him together as a community and give him our most undivided attention. By far we do this best when we join our hearts and minds in total worship at a formal worship service. Bottom line and very simply put, we worship him the best when we go to church and worship him in the company of our fellow brothers and sisters.

To say we can worship him equally as well on the golf course as we can in church is simply not true.

To say that we can praise him just as well while we are out in a boat fishing on a nice, warm, sunshiny Sunday morning . . . it may sound like a good ploy to tell others; still we really do know better. It simply cannot, nor will it, be done.

To say we can praise and worship him just as well in the comfort of our own bed rather than getting up on a cold Sunday morning to attend church is something that as adults, we really do know is not the case either, regardless of whom we are trying to convince otherwise.

As I stated in an earlier chapter, based on a Gallup Poll conducted in June of 2004, only 43% of those who profess to be a member of a church or synagogue attended their respective services during the week prior to the survey. That means that 57% chose not to devote as much as even an hour or so of that entire week to the worship of our God at a formal worship service. Almost 6 out of every 10 of us made the free and intentional choice not to give our God our undivided attention and hold him in awe for even one hour that week by the joining together of our hearts and minds in total worship with our fellow brother and sisters.

Why is that? Why is it, that for us who live in this great land of ours, with all the blessings that we have been given, and with so much that we have to be thankful for, we as a society are not attending church as we should be today? This goes across the lines of all denominations. Catholics and Protestants alike are not being faithful to the worshiping of their God as we should be. As a society, for one reason or another, we have slipped. While we can use all types of excuses and attempt to rationalize in our minds as to why we are not attending, the bottom line is that we need to remember just who it is that we are failing to worship.

We do not attend worship services for the personal gratification of the priest or minister. We do not attend worship services for the satisfaction of others in the congregation or the growth of the parish or community. Nor do we attend worship services so a talented and gifted choir or musicians can entertain us. When it really boils right down to it, we are not even at worship services primarily so we can "*get*" something out of it." We are there to "*give*" not primarily to "*get*" and the reason that we are there to only "*give*" is because we already "*got*." God has already blessed us with so very much, including the most momentous of blessing, his only begotten Son. For us to even think that he "owes" us is a ludicrous thought. We attend worship services above all to *worship our God, who is God, because he is God.* C.S. Lewis once wrote:

> As long as you notice, and have to count the steps, you are not yet dancing but only learning to dance. A good shoe is a shoe you don't notice. Good reading becomes possible when you need not consciously think about eyes, or light, or print, or spelling. The perfect church service would be one we were almost unaware of; our attention would have been on God.

We have become very much of a consumerism society, in need of constant entertainment, and those attitudes have filtered over into our churches and the style and form of our worship. We are constantly approaching everything, including our worship services, on a basis of "What's in it for me?" or "What can I get out of it?" We fail to remember what worship is all about. It's more than simply being entertained. It's far more important than a simple "feel good" event.

We worship our God because of who our God is. In the 11th Chapter of Romans, we are reminded of this very fact when we read, "For from him and through him and for him all things are. To *him* be glory forever. Amen." [emphasis added] (Romans 11:36)

It will not only be impossible for us to keep God as the "Objective" of our lives, but our "Objective" will become almost meaningless unless we first develop, to its fullest degree possible, the gift of our desire to worship him on a continual and regular basis.

In the 89th Psalm we hear,

The heavens proclaim your wonders, O Lord, and your faithfulness, in the assembly of the holy ones. For who in the skies can rank with the Lord? Who is like the Lord among the sons of God? God is terrible in the council of the holy ones; he is great and awesome beyond all round and about him. O Lord, God of host, who is like you? Mighty are you O Lord, and your faithfulness surrounds you. (Psalm 89:6–9)

It is the worshiping of this God that is the one and only and single reason of why we attend worship services. To give him the worship that he is truly worthy of, we go to church and we worship in the company of our brothers and sisters.

It is our God that we worship and praise. The God who we hold as the "Objective" of our lives, that we also desire to have as our guide, as we put together our *Life's Strategic Plan.*

Our Faith Community of Believers

So far in this chapter, we have discussed how through personal and private prayer we build our relationship with our God. We have discussed how through time of solitude we learn to keep quiet for a change and just spend time with God, listening to Him, thus allowing our souls the precious and needed time to catch their breath. We also discussed the precious gift that our God has given to us through our inborn desire and need to worship him, and how we give to him the worship he is truly entitled to when we worship him in fellowship with our brothers and sisters in formal worship services in church.

In this final segment of this chapter, we will discuss the importance of active participation in a faith community and how the community plays an important role in the quality of one's *Life's Strategic Plan.*

From the very beginning of creation, the concept of community was been an important element in God's plan of salvation for his people. In Genesis, the very first book in the Bible, we hear one of the very first statements that God made to his most prized and cherished creation when he said, "It is not good for the man to be alone. I will make a suitable partner for him." (Genesis 2:18) From that time on, we see how God has continually down through time involved his people in community so they could and would work, worship, and be together.

From the Book of Exodus we hear of numerous events when God called his people together as a community. In the twelfth chapter of Exodus, we hear how an announcement went out to the *whole community* with the instructions on proper sacrifice (Exodus 12:3). Then a bit later in the same chapter of Exodus, we hear the instructions that, "The *whole community* of Israel *must keep this feast.*" [emphasis added] (Exodus 12:47) Still again in Exodus, we hear the call Moses made to Aaron when he said, "Tell the *whole* Israelite *community*: Present yourself before the Lord . . ." [emphasis added] (Exodus 16:9) In this very early book of the Bible, God continually called his people together as a community, for he knew how his people could and would benefit from the involvement of a community of believers.

Then in Book of Ezra, we hear how *the whole community came together to offer their gifts* at the time of the dedication of the Temple (Ezra 6:16–18). For God's community of believers, the Temple became the focal point for the gathering of his community for worship.

Then Jesus came on the scene, and the first thing he did after he returned from his 40 days of solitude in the desert following his baptism was to form a community. Each of the Gospels tells of how Jesus formed his small community of the Twelve Apostles as the beginning of his church. Even Jesus, in his own ministry, knew the benefits that the support of a loving community would bring to him, and that the concept of community would be an aid to him in the carrying out the will of his Father.

As Jesus provided insight and training to his apostles, he also taught them that their ministry would be much more effective if they tried not to go it on their own. In the sixth chapter of Mark, we hear that Jesus sent them out into the world with the power and authority to cast out the evil spirits, heal the sick, and make the blind see and the lame walk. Even with that tremendous power and authority given to them directly by God himself through the person of Jesus, he still knew the wisdom of community, so he sent them out "two by two."

Then in the 16th Chapter of Matthew, we hear Jesus, in preparation for the day that he would no longer be physically on this earth, formally establishing his church when we said to Peter, "I for my part declare to you, you are 'Rock' and upon this rock I will build my church, and the jaws of death shall not prevail against it. I will entrust to you the keys of the kingdom of heaven. Whatever you declare bound on earth shall be bound in heaven; whatever you declare loosed on earth shall be loosed in heaven." (Matthew 16:18–19) With those words to Peter, Jesus established *his* church. *His* community. A community that is so important to him that he said that *nothing*, absolutely *nothing*, including all the powers of Hell, could ever do anything to destroy it. That is how important his community was, and still is to him. That is how important he knew *his* community would be to *his* people.

In the second chapter of the Acts of the Apostles, we read how the Church, which is the community that Christ himself had established, had grown from the very beginning with the help of the Holy Spirit, for we hear,

> Those who accepted his message were baptized; some three thousand were added that day. They devoted themselves to the apostles' instructions and the communal life, to the breaking of bread and prayers . . . Day by day the Lord added to their number those who were being saved (Acts 2:41–42; 47a).

Repeatedly throughout the New Testament, the importance of the community that Christ had established was continually confirmed. In the First Chapter of Ephesians, we hear, "He has put all things under Christ's feet and has made him, thus exalted, head of the church, which is his body: the fullness of him who fills the universe in all its parts." (Ephesians 1:22–23) No greater importance or prominence could our God give to the community he had established. He has told us that it is *in his community, his church,* that we will experience his true presence. In the Gospel of Matthew we hear the very words of Christ himself when he says, "Where two or three are gathered in my name, there am I in their midst." (Matthew 18:20)

So we do have concrete, undisputable proof from Scripture of the importance that Christ himself placed on the community that he had established here on earth. In spite of all the mistakes that we as humans can sometimes make, we also have the comforting assurance directly from him that, "the jaws of death shall not prevail against it," (Matthew 16:18b) and the further comforting assurance of his promise when he told us, "And know that I am with you always, until the end of the world." (Matthew 28:20b)

It is through his community that we find the support and fellowship we need in order for us to truly keep our eyes fixed on him as the "Objective" of life. It is through our active participation with his community that our faith remains alive and is nurtured and given to growth. Reverend Billy Graham once said, "Church-goers are like coals in a fire. When they cling together, they keep the flame aglow; when they separate, they die out."

We have absolute proof of how important his community is to him. When we add to that proof all the concrete benefits there are for all of all us who profess to be his followers, why is it, then, that in our society today we find that church membership and active participation is slipping? Earlier I cited a Gallup Poll that indicated that of those who claim a belief in God, only 67% consider themselves as members of a church or synagogue. That figure even includes all those who are only "card-carrying" members. While I have not seen any recent statistics, I would imagine, however, that if all those who are members in name only would be eliminated from the rosters, the figure would change drastically.

In the world we live in today, especially as fast-paced, hectic, chaotic, and stressful as our lives can be at times, our need for the support we can get from each other in our individual Christian communities is as great, if not even greater, than it has ever been.

In so many other segments of our society, we have discovered the benefits of joining together as a community. Memberships at gyms and fitness centers have never been greater. While any of us, at most any time, with little or no cost, can exercise right in our own homes in a wide variety of ways, we still pay to join a gym or fitness center, and we do so because it's a proven fact that we do better and enjoy it more when we have the support of others who have a similar goal.

Weight-loss organizations are popping up all over the place. In spite of all the new ones, most of those who have been around for a number of years are also experiencing ever-increasing membership. Why? Any of us have the ability to push ourselves away from the table and not continue to eat. Government nutrition policies give us the calorie and fat content of virtually anything we consume, so we don't really need the help of such an organization to tell us *what or how much* to eat. But they are growing because of the success members experience as a result of the encouragement and support they receive from others in the community.

There is a long list of such groups - Alcoholics Anonymous, Gamblers Anonymous, and Parents without Partner, just to name a few - where people who are members of a community can find encouragement, support and success in their endeavors in a way that would never be possible without their community. Yet when it comes to our most important focus, the focus of our faith and the God who must be the true "Objective" of our lives, we often have a tendency to feel that we can "go it alone" without the assistance and support of a community.

Editor for the Gallup Organization, Albert Winseman, states in an article in *Religious and Social Trends for the Gallup Organization*, that based on a survey conducted in late 2003, an individual's *level* of congregational engagement is a significant factor in his or her likelihood to be spiritually committed. He said that 39% who are *actively engaged* members of their congregations are also fully spiritually committed. That compares to only 9% of the members who are not engaged, and only 4% of those who are disengaged.[35]

He further stated that those who were *active*

and participating members of their respective faith communities overwhelmingly gave a response of "strongly agree" to each of the nine items that Gallup has determined best measure spiritual commitment. These nine items are:

- I spend time in worship or prayer every day.

- My faith is involved in every aspect of my life.

- Because of my faith, I have forgiven people who have hurt me deeply.

- Because of my faith, I have meaning and purpose in my life.

- My faith has caused me to develop my given strengths.

- I will take unpopular stands to defend my faith.

- My faith gives me an inner peace.

- I speak words of kindness to those in need of encouragement.

- I am a person who is spiritually committed.

also invite you to re-read the chapter on happiness and then re-read the nine points as mentioned above from the article on spiritual commitment written by Albert Winseman of the Gallup Organization, and then let's talk further.

Or how about the statement, *"I just can't find a religion that I feel I can grow in."*? To that statement I offer two comments for consideration. The first is that anyone who says they cannot find an authentic Christian religion or Christian faith community that does not fit their needs is really not looking too hard. With the hundreds, indeed thousands, of congregations in the United States today, if you can't find one that agrees with you, then chances are you are not looking for a religion, what you are looking for may be some kind of a mutual admiration society. This brings me to the second comment I would like to make. Any religion that has its focus on meeting every whim or desire of society is not a religion at all—it's a popularity contest—it's a be all things to all people type of church, without any foundation in Scripture or Sacred Tradition. The job and purpose of religion is not to bend to the whims and secular desires of society; rather, its purpose is to be a voice with an attempt to keep society straight.

One last statement that is often used: *"I'm an inactive member."* Actually that's an oxymoron. It's a total contradiction in and of itself. One simply cannot be an inactive member of a community. By definition, if one is a part of the community, he or she must be involved and active with the other members of the community. If you're no longer involved, then you are no longer a member. You may be an ex-member, or a former member, or even a lapsed member, but you simply cannot be a member who is simply inactive.

If you say, for example, that you're a Lutheran, then be a Lutheran and be a part of their faith community. If you say you're a Catholic, then be a Catholic and be a part of their faith community. If you say you're a member of a non-congregational community, then be a part of it and be active with them.

To be a member of a faith community requires being more than just an occasional attendee, or worse than even that, being a card carrying member in name only. Being a member requires being part of the family and being active in that family.

If one is truly serious about their desire to keep their God as the "Objective" of their life, then full and active participation in their respective faith community is a must. Any plan of life that does not include that of being an active member of your faith community is, at best, an incomplete plan.

Benediction

May God, the source of all patience
and encouragement,
enable you to live in perfect harmony with one another
according to the spirit of Christ Jesus,
so that with one heart and voice
you may glorify God,
the Father of our Lord Jesus Christ.
Accept once another, then, as Christ
accepted you, for the glory of God.

(Romans 15:5–7)

chapter ten

Life's Strategic Plan

Now that we have discussed several of the basic elements and factors that will have an impact on our achieving the life we desire, it is now time for us to focus on the task of actually putting together your *Life's Strategic Plan.*

In this chapter, you will be presented with a method for putting on paper, in a clear and concise manner, a description and plan for the life you wish to have. Then and even more importantly, you will be given suggestions on how to make your plan become a reality.

It's important to remember that our purpose in this chapter is not to put together your professional goals, or even the personal goals for the things you would like to *have* in life. This is not a goal-setting session in the sense of determining where you want your career to go or how much money you wish to earn.

This session is intended to have its major focus on your life in the sense of *"being,"* with only a minor focus on the *"doing."* For as we discussed earlier, our true happiness, fulfillment, and gratification in life is especially found in *who* we are much more than in what we *do*.

By giving your *Life's Strategic Plan* intentional and serious thought and consideration, and then by following through with the implementation of your plan, you will reap the following benefits:

- It will help determine whether any of your professional or personal goals are in conflict with you becoming the person you really desire to become.

- It will give you a focus and peace of mind such as you may have never experienced before.

- You will use your mind and talents more fully with more focus on the *"being"* rather than simply the *"doing."*

- Your life will be focused on the direction you are moving instead of just where you may be today.

- Because you will have a better view of the big picture, you will find yourself making better life decisions.

- You will have more control over your life. You will find it easier to prioritize what is important, and then find yourself more effective and productive regarding what is important.

- You will find more gratification and fulfillment in what you are doing in life,
  both personally and professionally, thus
  giving you greater confidence and self-
  worth.

- You will be more enthusiastic and moti-
  vated to live life to the fullest.

- You will find it easier to use the gifts and
  talents with which God had blessed you
  to accomplish projects you never thought
  possible. His grace will be fully alive in
  your life as never before.

Putting together this plan is serious business.
After all, it's your life that you're planning. What we
are about to accomplish is a lot more that putting a
few words, concepts, or neat ideas down on paper.
This exercise is far more serious, and for sure more
fruitful, than putting together a few New Year's Res-
olutions. What we are doing here is serious planning.
What we are doing is serious work. According to
United States Governments Small Business Administration, only 3% of Americans ever spend time
in putting together goals for life. Doing this exercise puts you ahead and gives you a better chance
to experience the happiness you desire than 97% of
your fellow citizens.

To do this serious work, it is absolutely necessary that you be able to give it your undivided atten-

tion. If now is not the best time for you to give this important work the attention that is required and necessary, then determine when a more suitable time would be. If you are serious about your plan, you will set aside the time needed to accomplish this all-important task. But don't use the excuse that you do not have the time to do it. Remember, time is one of the impediments that often keep us from having the life we desire. Time is just another excuse used by the other 97%. Don't let that excuse prevent you from putting together your *Life's Strategic Plan.* I remind you once again of the wisdom spoken by Mark Twain when he said, "Plan for the future, because that's where you are going to spend the rest of your life."

So if the time is right, and if you're ready to put together your *Life's Strategic Plan*, then roll up your sleeves, grab a pen and paper (or your lap-top) and let's go to work.

Exercise #1

We need to reconfirm in our mind, and without any hesitation or limitation, that our God is the "Objective" of our life. Any of our plans that do not include our Creator as our "Objective" are not workable plans that will have any lasting value or benefit. Everything that we include in our plan must point back to our God and his will. If there is anything not in complete compliance and in full alignment with God's will and plan for our salvation, then it must be eliminated immediately, since it will only prove to be a point of frustration, ultimate disappointment, and sadness.

So to complete this first exercise, we must pause in quiet meditation, and, each in his own way, call upon the name of our God and ask him to send His Holy Spirit to be with you and guide you as you undertake the important task of putting together your *Life's Strategic Plan.*

So we now begin with the full faith and confidence that the Holy Spirit is with us.

Exercise #2

The first step in putting together your *Life's Strategic Plan* is to carefully review your current life and lifestyle. Before you can envision a new life, you first need a full and complete understanding of all the assets, liabilities, and encumbrances that are currently a part of your life.

Knowing and understanding your *assets* is important, for they often consist of the gifts and talents with which God has blessed you. An asset can only develop into its true value when it is recognized, understood, and then allowed to grow and flourish so to bring the happiness and meaning to one's life to the degree that God had intended.

Knowing and understanding your *liabilities* is important, for they often consist of the areas in your life that if not recognized and admitted to, can prevent you from having the life you desire and the happiness in this life for which God has designed for you. Not all liabilities can be eliminated, however.

Once they are recognized, understood, and admitted to, it usually becomes possible to design *Life's Strategic Plan* in such a manner that will enable one to maneuver around it.

Knowing and understanding our *encumbrances* is important, as they often consist of all those little obstacles that seem to creep into our everyday life. These are obstacles that can have an adverse affect on our attitudes as well as our general outlook of what life was really meant to be. Until obstacles are recognized and understood to be nothing more than what they really are, we can often escalate them in our mind to the point that they can become a major liability.

One good way to take an inventory of your life and lifestyle is to review each of the basic topics as discussed in this book. By doing so, it will assist you in making an honest discernment of some of the assets, liabilities, and/or encumbrances in your life. So for this examination and review, the answers to the following questions will provide a general place to start. You may discover other questions or even other areas of discernment that may apply to your individual life. But as stated, this is a place to start.

The "What" Factor

- Do I feel that my current career or profession is my true calling in life?
- Do I honestly feel that through what I am doing in my professional life, I am able to utilize the gifts and talents with which

God has blessed me? If so, list each of those gifts and talents. If not, list the gifts and talents that you are prevented from using, or do not use.

- If you could have any job or profession in life that you wanted, would it include your current job or profession? If not, what would you change?
- Can you honestly say that you love and enjoy your profession or career, and do you look forward to getting out of bed in the morning to go to work?

The "How Factor"

- What priority does my profession or career have in the total scheme of my life?
- How much of what I do in life defines who I am as a person?
- Would I admit that I am "obsessed" with my profession or career, and if so, is it the greatest obsession I have in my life?
- How would my spouse, children, or close friends answer the above question?
- If either you or others would describe you as being obsessed with your profession or career, then describe that obsession in detail. Is it a matter of power, money, prestige, position of honor, the pride of accomplishment, or the adrenalin of the chase?

- Do you feel that you keep your job or profession in the perspective that God meant it to be?
- How would your spouse, children, or a close friend answer the above question?

Stewardship

- Do I recognize all my time, talents, and treasures as gifts from God?
- Do I agree with the statement that God expects for us to be responsible stewards for everything with which we have been blessed?
- Do I have an "Attitude of Gratitude" for all I have been blessed with, and if so, by the life I live, how would *God* recognize that attitude?
- How does my being a good steward of all God's gifts enhance my spirituality and relationship with God?
- How does my spirituality of stewardship help to define who I am as a human *being*?

Establishing Priorities

- Have I ever reduced my life's priorities to writing?
- Do I have the priorities of my life in their right order?
- Do the actions of my daily life reflect the priorities I say I have?

- How would my spouse, my children, or good friends answer those questions?

The Proverbial Rat Race

- Do I have control of my schedule, or do I let my schedule control me?
- Does my daily schedule permit me to live the life I feel God has called me to?
- Does my typical schedule make me feel frazzled and testy or organized and fulfilled?
- Do I often miss important events or appointment because I did not plan my schedule, or did not plan appropriately according to my priorities?
- Is my typical schedule a cause for stress and anxiety, and if so, does it adversely affect my work, my relationships, and my spirituality?
- Do I sometimes use the excuse of "not having enough time" for not living my life according to the priorities I say have?

It's Past our Bedtime

- Am I able to get the amount of sleep I am in need of?
- Is my lack of sleep having an adverse affect on my work, my relationships, and my spirituality?
- Am I finding that I sometimes make stu-

pid mistakes due to being too tired?

- Am I finding that my lack of sleep adversely affects my productivity and alertness?
- Because of my lack of sleep, am I finding myself more susceptible to illness?
- Is my lack of sleep affecting my attitude and enthusiasm toward a full and productive life?
- Is my lack of ample sleep primarily my own fault for not having a proper routine or schedule?

We Just Need to Take a Little Break

- Do I find myself with feelings of exhaustion for long periods of time?
- Is my exhaustion adversely affecting my morale, enthusiasm, and even self-esteem?
- Is my state of exhaustion affecting the energy I am willing or able to put forth toward the things I hold to be important?
- Is my state of exhaustion forcing me to change some of my priorities?
- Do I often find myself exhausted to the point that it adversely affects my relationships and/or my ability to enjoy life?
- Is my state of exhaustion often making me feel "burned-out?"

"As We Forgive Those Who Trespass Against Us"

- Am I carrying a grudge against someone who has done me wrong?
- Does my blood begin to boil, or do my nerves and muscles tighten whenever I think of this person and the manner in which I was hurt?
- Do I want revenge for the pain I received?
- Is my failure to forgive due to my inability or my unwillingness?
- How would my life be different if I would not have been hurt in the way I was?
- How would my life change if I were to grant forgiveness to that one person who has hurt me the most and then be able to go on with life?

The Stress of Everyday Life

- Are the stressors in my life a cause to energize and encourage me to a more full and productive life, or are they a cause for feelings of depression, anxiety, short temper, and worry?
- Are the stressors in my life adversely affecting my relationships, my work, and my spirituality?
- What control do I have over the stressors in my life?

- What steps can I take to eliminate the major negative stressors in my life?
- In order to reduce some of the negative stress in my life, do I practice any of the suggestions as offered by the National Mental Health Association that are outlined in Chapter 8 of this book?

Problems of Everyday Life

- How do I typically react to the everyday problems of life?
- What percentage of my conversation with others is spent in discussing my problems?
- When someone tells me of their problem, do I feel the need to tell them of my problems that are, in my opinion, bigger or worse then theirs?
- What percentage of my problems do I feel are *not* caused due to my own actions or decisions?
- How often do I play the "poor me" game and want to invite others to my own personal "pity party"?

Worry

- How often do I worry about those things I have no control over?
- How much time do I spend worrying about things that *might* happen?
- How often does worry affect my ability

to get a good night's sleep?
- How does my worry affect my ability to smile, laugh, and enjoy life?
- Does my worry often prevent me from having a positive and optimistic outlook on the future?

Personal & Private Prayer

- Do I have what I feel is a quality personal prayer life?
- Do I spend time each day in personal prayer?
- How much of my prayer is only of the "Lord grant me" or "Lord help me" type of prayer?
- Is my present personal prayer life enhancing my relationship with God?
- Is prayer important and meaningful in my life?
- Does my prayer life bring God into my life on a personal and intimate level, or do I have the feeling that he is just "somewhere out there."

Solitude

- Have I ever devoted an extended period of time for solitude with God?
- Is the relationship I desire with God deserving of a minimum of one 8-hour day per year as a time of solitude with him?

- How can and will time spent in solitude with God enhance the quality of my life and my pursuit of happiness?
- How can and will time spent in solitude with God enhance the quality of the relationships I have with my spouse, children, friends, and co-workers.

Worship

- Do I attend worship services on a regular and routine basis?
- For what reason do I attend worship services?
- What importance does attending and participating in worship services play in my pursuit of happiness?
- Do I typically attend worship services for the purpose of *giving* or *getting*?

Our Faith Community of Believers

- Am I a registered member of a Faith Community?
- What level of participation do I have in the life and vitality of my Faith Community?
- Do I look to my Faith Community more to *serve* or to *be served*?
- What role does my faith community play in my pursuit of happiness?
- What benefits do I expect to receive as being a member of a Faith Community?

- How can my Faith Community strengthen my ability to give my God the praise and glory he is due?
- How can my Faith Community assist me in helping to build the Kingdom of God?

Exercise #3

In the previous exercise, we reviewed the life we now have. In this exercise we want to create the vision of what we want our lives to be. As was discussed in Chapter 5, without a clear vision of the life we desire, all our hopes and dreams for the future may be nothing more than mere empty wishes—wishes that we have without any degree of faith and/or confidence in the possibility of us ever achieving the life that we are in search of.

Christ told us that he wanted for us to be all that we can be for the glory of his name when he said,

> I came that they might have life and have it to the full . . . I am the vine and you are the branches. He who lives in me and I in him, will produce abundantly, for apart from me you can do nothing . . . It was not you who chose me, it was I who chose you to go forth and bear much fruit . . . (John 10:10b; 15:5; 16a)

And so it is with that faith and confidence that we set our pen to paper to create the vision of what we desire our lives to be.

Remember, this exercise is about creating the vision for the type of *life* you desire. It is not about setting the goals for life; that will come in a later exercise. Before we can even think about setting our goals, we first need to have a desired destination. We'll worry about how we're going to get there later.

In this exercise, you are asked to spend as much time as you need to write out, in paragraph form, a complete narrative of all that you want your life to be. Include in your vision every aspect of both your personal and professional life. Remember this is not a time for establishing personal or business goals, rather this narrative should provide a clear and concise vision statement of what you want your *life* to be.

Include in your detailed vision statement a description of the relationships that you have, or would like to have in your life. Include relationships with both family and friends. Remember, the key secret here is in the details, so include every detail you can think of for what you would like for your personal life to be. For example, say you would like to lose some weight; the details of your vision statement should include not only how much weight you desire to lose, but more importantly, how you think you will feel both physically and emotionally after your loss of weight. Or maybe that detail would include not only what size of clothing you *will* be wearing, but also describe the positive affect that wearing that size of clothing will have on your life.

If it is a habit you would like to break, then describe not only the habit, but also describe in detail what life would be like *without* having that habit as a constant part of your life.

Maybe your vision statement will include a new home, a new car, or having less debt or more money in savings. If so, write it out in complete detail. If it's a new home, for example, go so far as to describe the home as you would to a friend as if you already live in it. Go so far as to even describe the neighborhood. But more than describing the bricks and mortar of the house or the neighborhood, it's even more important that you describe your life as a result of living in this house or neighborhood.

Remember, this exercise is about the *life* you desire, not about the *things* you desire. But again, details, details, details is the key. So describe it until you can envision it.

Also keep in mind that this is your own personal worksheet. It's not an assignment that you will be turning in to be graded or reviewed. So be as creative as you desire. But also remember, this is not a "make a wish fairy tale." This is your *Life's Strategic Plan,* so it is absolutely necessary that you can truly envision having the life that you are describing in your vision statement.

Include also in your vision statement a full description of your professional life and how you see yourself spending almost one-third of your life. Again, remember that this is not a time for business planning or setting the goals of what you want to accomplish in your career. This is a vision of your life with a focus on the *"being"* and not the *"doing."* As such, your vision statement should have its focus on what you will *"be,"* not what or how much you will *"do."* Again, remember the details, so describe your professional life in as vivid detail as you can. Describe it so you can envision what your life will be like in the profession or job you *will* be in. Your description may be of your current profession or career, or maybe not. In addition to the type of job or career, you may even want to include a description of, or even the name of the company you will be working for. Maybe this will be your current company, or maybe not.

Include how you see yourself involved in your church and/or faith community. Describe the religious practices and traditions that are, or will be, a part of your life. Describe the name and location of the congregation you belong to. Describe what it means for you to be a member of this congregation. Again, don't forget the details. Maybe your vision statement describes your involvement with the community or how you support the community in other ways. Describe how the involvement in your religion and faith community is entwined in other areas of your life. Again, describe not only the *"doing"* part of your faith and your involvement in your faith community, but more importantly, describe what your life will *"be"* as a result of what you are *doing*.

In this area of your vision statement, make certain that what you write is not simply a feel good, clear-my-conscience type of essay. Remember, this is your *Life's Strategic Plan.* If you cannot envision it as fact and reality, then don't write it. You do not want your plan to be a *make believe fair tale.*

In each of the individual areas of your vision statement above, be sure to include your timetables, and again, this should be in complete detail. If, for example, your personal plan calls for more education or a different job sometime in the future, then include the date by which you will start it. Give detail to your date. Don't simply state that you will achieve whatever it may be in three years. Rather, include the specific date for its achievement. If three years from now is the year 2009, then that is what you should write. By including the specific date, it permits you to arrive at a detailed plan that will help you to envision yourself actually obtaining it.

Include in your vision how, through the life you desire, you will be able to use the gifts and talents with which you have been blessed to be the person God intends for you to be. Most importantly, include with a sense of certainty how the life, as you have described it, will not only permit you, but more importantly, will encourage you to keep your God as the "Objective" of your life.

Write and rewrite your vision statement as many times as necessary until you have every detail included. For it will be in the details that you will obtain a clear vision of the life you desire. Ideally, this should take more than one sitting to do. Once you have completed the first draft, it's a good idea to put it to the side and think about it for at least a day. When you return to it, thoroughly re-read it one more time and make any changes you feel necessary.

If upon re-reading it you feel that your emotions or enthusiasm may have become a bit too creative the first time around and you now cannot envision the life you had described in the first draft, then by all means, change it. If you cannot envision that life after only a single day, then chances are it was never a true vision in the first place, but rather only a wish. However, don't be shy about asking or dreaming of the unthinkable. Let your dreams flourish about the life you want. Remember the words of St. Paul in his Letter to the Ephesians when he wrote, "To him whose power now at work in us can do immeasurably more than we ask or imagine." (Ephesians 3:20) God wants us to live to the fullest the life he has given us. His desire is for us to use all the gifts and talents with which he has blessed us to become all that we can be for the honor and glory of His Holy Name. He assured us that by his power at work within us, we will accomplish far more than we could possibly ever ask or imagine.

Oliver Wendel Holmes said, "The mind, once expanded to the dimension of larger ideas, never returns to its original size." So expand your mind and describe with as much vivid detail as you can the vision of the life you desire. Again, take your time and be serious about it.

Exercise #4

Now from your vision statement, and in a grocery list format, make a list of all the benefits that you envision that the life you want will provide to you compared to the life you now have. This is an important part of your plan, since not only must we be able envision the life we want, but we must also be able to envision the benefits of that life, and how those benefits will improve the quality of our lives and enhance our happiness. It may also provide you with some insight as to the quality of the life and the blessings that you already have.

Exercise #5

Now we go back again to Exercise #3 and the vision of your life. Again, in a grocery list format, make a list of everything that you must have or need to accomplish before that life can be yours. If you need additional education, for example, write that down. If a relationship is what is desired, then describe in detail what you need to do in order to achieve that relationship. Whatever it is that is preventing you from having the life that you desire, write it down.

Again, this list must be in complete detail. For example, if part of what you desire in your future life requires education, then don't just list it by simply making the statement, "I need more education." But rather, make your statement complete so as to include every detail. Again using education as the example, your statement may be something like, "I need to further my education by getting my _____ degree or diploma. This will take about _____ years to complete and will cost _____ dollars."

At this time don't be concerned with how you are going to get what you're going to need; just list the needs in detail.

Exercise #6

Now review each of the items on the list you made in Exercise #5 and then determine what, if any, task, obstacle, or sacrifice that must be overcome or accomplished before it can be achieved. For example: using the education scenario, maybe some of the task, obstacles, or sacrifices you may have to overcome could be:

1)   Your need for money or a scholarship for tuition and books.

2)   Your current work schedule will have to be adjusted. Is that a possibility? If not, what are the alternatives that will need to be implemented before your educational needs can be pursued?

3)   What effect will your desire or need for further education have on other commitments you may already have, especially your commitments and obligations to your family or your work? What adjustments will need to be made, and what affect will those adjustments have not

only on your life, but also on the lives of others?

It's important that you meticulously list in as vivid detail as possible each and every task, obstacle, or sacrifice you will have to overcome. Failure to give thoughtful consideration of each and every possibility is like planning a trip and forgetting to give consideration as to the type of transportation you will be using.

It's important to remember that obstacles and/ or sacrifices on your path are not necessarily roadblocks; they are only obstacles that may require sacrifice, thoughtful consideration, and a determination to overcome. With a clear vision of a successful outcome and a solid and firm faith in your ability to achieve the life you desire, you will discover there are very few obstacles or sacrifices that you will not be able to be overcome.

Exercise #7

Now in this, Exercise #7, you will review each of the items you listed in Exercise #6, and then for each item, arrive at a concise and detailed plan of how each one *can* and *will* be accomplished. In your detailed plan, list not only how it can be accomplished, but also state the time required, or at least the time you are allowing for its accomplishment.

Once completed, then determine whether the sacrifices required to overcome any of the obstacles are at a higher price than you are willing or able to pay, or if the sacrifice is such that it creates a problem or dilemma that may adversely affect other areas of your life that have a higher priority.

If any item conflicts with another part of your life, especially one at a higher priority, then common sense will tell you that it's time to go back to the drawing board, for that part of your desired future is not realistic, at least not at this point in time. The fact is, if we cannot envision how we can first overcome the obstacles, we certainly will not be able to clearly envision, with any degree of faith or confidence, the final outcome that we desire for our lives.

The decision of "go" or "no go" on any goal of life must be a personal decision that only you can make. They cannot be the goals your parents may have for you, or even goals a spouse would like for you to have. If the goals you are after in life, are not, in true fact, your own goals that lead you to the life you desire, then they are worthless.

Having said that, however, if you are married, you must make your final decision only after full consultation with your spouse. Two people who are committed as one in life must not grow apart by each going down their own separate roads, especially roads that may be in conflict with each other. This is not meant to imply that both spouses should have identical vision statements; quite the contrary. As individuals, each party should have a clear vision of their own life. It is saying, however, that the two vision statements should not include areas or items that are in conflict with each other. For example, if the vision statement of one includes a life in a Manhattan high-rise condo and the other is a life in a rustic log cabin deep in the woods of Michigan, then chances are there may be a conflict that needs some discussion.

Or let's use one that may be a bit more practical. Say that each spouse desires additional education, and both are envisioning taking night classes to accomplish this. Now if there are children, and childcare is a necessity, then this is an item that will need some discussion between the two, or there could be a conflict.

Remember, it's a lot easier to work with the current of life than against it. Couples who are not working in unison for a life together are like trying to swim up stream in a fast current.

Exercise #8

In Exercise #8, our job is to prioritize our goals. Our first priority list will separate our goals into short term and long term goals, with short term being defined as those to be accomplished within 12 months or less, and the rest as long-term. Again, remember that every goal, both short-term and long-term, must lead us to the life we desire and had described in our visionary statement in Exercise #3 above.

Once we have each goal identified as either short-term or long-term, we now will list them in order of priority as we want them to happen, and we begin by prioritizing our long-term goals. For each long-term goal we must have a corresponding short-term goal that will lead us closer to achieving our long-term goal.

We can again use the scenario of the educational goal. If our goal is to earn a specific degree in the next 3–4 years, then our short-term goals must include goals determining when we are going to begin classes, what classes we will take during the first 12 months, and exactly when those classes will begin. If cost is a consideration, then we need to detail the source of those funds. Likewise, if your goal is to earn the degree in 8 years, then you must have a short term goal of exactly what you are going to do *this year* to get you there. If you do not have an identified short-term goal to accomplish your desired long-term goal, then the goal is no goal; and I'll say it again, it's only a fairy tale wish.

Additionally, it is absolutely vital that one goal must never conflict with another. For example, if one of your goals is to put aside a given amount of money into a savings account or a retirement plan and another is to make a large purchase, and your income does not provide for the accomplishing of both, then they would be in conflict with each other. Assuming that there are no provisions for additional income, a decision must then be made as to which will take priority and which will be put off until *a later time.*

Exercise # 9

Once we have both our short-term and long-term goals identified and prioritized, it is now necessary for us to take one last review of not only each goal individually, but also all our goals that we have established as a whole. By this review, we need to once again determine if we can literally envision the accomplishing of each. This is not to say that goals should not be challenging, as they should be, but the first requirement is that you must have faith in your ability to accomplish each of them. If you cannot first conceive and believe in them, you will never be able to achieve them.

Another important part of Exercise #9 is to make the final determination on whether the goals you have established will indeed move you toward the life you desire. And most importantly, will that life that you desire and can envision move you to a greater love of God, neighbor, and the world, or will it edge you toward isolation and apathy? It's time now to make the final determination as to whether the goals you have established will solve problems and create opportunity and happiness in your life or create only new problems and add additional chaos in your life.

The final determination as to whether our goal is a worthy goal or not will be based on whether or not the working toward our goal, as well as the accomplishing of it, will help us keep our focus on God as the true "Objective" of our life.

Exercise #10

In this final exercise, we will formalize the vision statement of your *Life's Strategic Plan*. We will pull together all the information that we have prayed about, thought about, written and rewritten, adjusted, erased, added to, and prioritized in the previous nine exercises. So with pen and paper (or the lap-top), we begin by writing out in complete detail your *Life's Strategic Plan* as we can envision that plan in living Technicolor.

So you can take ownership of your plan, we naturally begin with the title. So at the top of the page, center in bold letters the title of *My Life's Strategic Plan.* Under the title, place your name as the author, and under your name, place the date. So then, your title page would look something like this:

My Life's Strategic Plan
Your Name
Today's Date

This next part of this exercise is very similar in nature and style to that of the vision statement you had written in Exercise # 3 above. The main difference, however, is that it is to be much shorter in length, but yet not any less descriptive, for this new abbreviated narrative shall become the mission statement of your life. As your mission statement, it becomes the summary focus for you to attain the *life* you are envisioning. Your life's mission statement should have a focus on your *being* in life, not your *doing.* Your mission statement should provide a clear description of your life's mission to become the person you wish to become and to have the life you desire. It should not focus or describe what you want to do in life or what you would like to have or achieve in life.

Once you have your mission statement completed, your next task is to now focus on what you need to do in order to be the type of person you want to be, and experience the happiness in this life that you are in pursuit of. While it is true that throughout this book we emphatically preached the importance of the need to focus on the *being* and not on the *doing*, it is in the doing that you can take control of your life and use the gifts and talents with which God has so blessed you in order to become the person he intends for you to be. Building the Kingdom of God is no spectator sport. You have been given all the tools necessary to become that person and to live the life that God had intended specifically for you, as one of his prized and cherished creations. So with that in mind, we now begin to assemble our long and short term goals.

The next part of this exercise is to be completed in a traditional outline format, so we begin with the Roman Numeral One. Next to that number, we write the long term goal that we have established as having our highest priority. Remember, a long term goal is one that will take longer than twelve months to achieve. The writing of this goal can and should be stated in as few words as necessary, and it should be written in all capital letters.

For the purpose of providing an illustration of the proper format, I will use the example of a person having the desire to obtain additional education as one of their primary long-term goals. Additionally, we'll use the assumption that you are writing this in the year of 2006 and you envision that it will take two years to get everything in place before you can begin classes, and then another four years to get your degree. Therefore, with this in mind, we continue with our *Life's Strategic Plan* by adding the first Roman numeral, after which we state our goal. Upon completing it, your plan would begin to look something like this:

My Life's Strategic Plan
Your Name
Today's Date

Insert here the narrative that has become your life's mission statement. It can be as short or as long as desired; however, it must be clear and descriptive so as to describe the life you desire and the happiness you are in pursuit of.

I. EARN MY DEGREE IN BUSINESS ADMINIS-
    TRATION
    Under your long-term goal, write one or two sentences that will identify both the school you will attend as well as the timetable you have established to obtain your degree. It may look like this:

I. EARN MY DEGREE IN BUSINESS ADMINIS-
    TRATION
    Beginning with the fall semester of 2009, I will be attending (*name of school)* and will obtain my degree by the spring of 2013.

Remember that for each long-term goal, it is necessary to have a corresponding short-term goal or goals that will lead to achieving of the long-term goal. And as stated earlier, a short-term goal is defined here as one that can be accomplished in twelve months or less. So to continue with our outline, your short-term goals relating to your long-term goal for education may look like this:

I. EARN MY DEGREE IN BUSINESS ADMINIS-
   TRATION
   Beginning with the fall semester of 2009 I will be attending _(name the school) and will obtain my degree by the spring of 2013.
   A. By the end of this year of 2006 I will have accomplished the following short-term goals that will lead me to achieving my long term goal:
      1. By the end of the March, I will make a visit to the college so I can meet with the admissions office in order to determine the requirements for admission, the cost, and the availability for financial aid.
      2. So I will have the necessary finances available for me to obtain my education, beginning in January I will deposit $____ from each and every paycheck into a special savings account, which I will designate and use specifically for my college fund.

Note that the two short-term goals as written in the illustration above are very date and detail specific. If one was to write the goal by simply stating "sometime this year I will check into what it will take to get enrolled" chances are that "sometime" will never come to pass. Likewise, if one was to state that they were going to save some money for college, chances are equally as good that that will never happen either. Be specific and be committed to it.

Continue in this same format by listing each and every short-term goal that will lead you to the accomplishing of your long-term goal.

Next, list as Roman Numeral Two the long term goal you have as your next highest priority, after which you list all your short-term goals relating to it.

Continue in the same manner until you have all your long-term goals listed in their appropriate order of priority, along with each correlating short-term goals.

While it is necessary that every long term goal must have correlating short term goals, there are, however, some goals that by their very nature are only short-term. While they must definitely help lead you to the life you desire, by themselves they are stand-alone short term goals.

Therefore, once you have all your long-term goals listed in their order of priority, after the next Roman numeral in sequence, write the words, MY SHORT TERM GOALS FOR THE YEAR OF 2006. Then in the same outline format, list each of your remaining short-term goals, in the order of the priority you have established.

Once completed, now add your final Roman Numeral, after which you will insert the words, "MY CONTINUED GOAL IS TO ALWAYS KEEP MY GOD AS THE 'OBJECTIVE' OF MY LIFE." This statement then becomes your last long range goal. The difference between how you state this goal compared to all the others is that it will have no completion date, for this is a lifetime goal. This long-term goal is one that you will continue to strive toward and improve upon for the rest of your life. Additionally, this will be your only long-term goal that will be out of sequence as to the order of its priority in your life. Although listed last, it is indeed the most important. We end with this as our final goal, for this is the one we desire to have as our lasting impression for our *Life's Strategic Plan*. Additionally, by having it as the last, it serves as a sort of a summary of everything else that will lead us to the life we desire and the happiness we are in pursuit of. It is with faith that we acknowledge that this is the most important Roman numeral of your *Life's Strategic Plan*. Once again, we recall the words of Christ when he said;

I am the vine and you are the branches. He who lives in me and I in him, *will produce abundantly*, for apart from me you can do nothing. My Father has been glorified in your bearing *much fruit* and becoming my disciples. [emphasis added] (John 15:5, 8)

As with all long-term goals, it is necessary that we have our short-term goals that will lead us to the accomplishing of the long-term. For this we will list those goals that will help us to accomplish our permanent long-term goal of keeping our God as the "Objective" of our life. These goals should consist of the primary areas of Personal Prayer, Solitude, Worship, Stewardship, and our participation in our Faith Community.

Now that you have completed your entire *Life's Strategic Plan,* you will find that the finish product will look something like this:

My Life's Strategic Plan
Your Name
Today's Date

In this area insert the narrative that has become your life's mission statement. It can be as short or as long you desire, however it must be clear and descriptive so as to describe the life you desire and the happiness you are in pursuit of.

I. EARN MY DEGREE IN BUSINESS ADMINIS-
   TRATION
   Beginning with the fall semester of 2009, I will be attending *(name the school)* and will obtain my degree by the spring of 2013.
   A. By the end of this year of 2006, I will
   have accomplished the following short-
   term goals that will lead me to achieving

my long term goal:

1. By the end of the March, I will make a visit to the college so I can meet with the admissions office in order to determine the requirements for admission, the cost, and the availability for financial aid.

2. So I will have the necessary finances available for me to obtain my education, beginning in January I will deposit $____ from each and every paycheck into a special savings account, which I will designate and use specifically for my college fund.

II. LONG TERM GOAL WITH THE NEXT HIGH-EST PRIORITY

A. Short-term goal that will lead to the accomplishing of the above long term-goal

III. LONG TERM GOAL WITH THE NEXT HIGH-EST PRIORITY

A. Short-term goal that will lead to the accomplishing of the above long term-goal

IV. MY SHORT TERM GOALS FOR THE YEAR OF 2006

The following goals are those I will accomplish during the next twelve months. The accomplishing of these goals will lead me to the life I desire.

A. By the end of the year, I will reduce my credit card balances by $_____.

    1. In addition to the minimum payment as requested by the credit card company, I will pay an additional amount of $_____ each and every month

    2. Additionally, each month I will pay 100% of whatever I charged during the month, and will charge no more than I am certain I can pay. Therefore, if I cannot pay it, I will not charge it.

B. Short-term goal number two

    1. Detailed plan to accomplish the above short term goal

V. MY CONTINUED GOAL IS TO ALWAYS KEEP MY GOD AS THE "OBJECTIVE" OF MY LIFE.

A. Personal Prayer

    1. Here you state your commitment to your daily personal prayer, and again, be as specific as you can.

B. Solitude

    1. State here your personal commitment as to the amount of time you are willing to commit to spending in Solitude with your God during this next year.

    2. State here *when* you will take this time. Be as date specific as possible.

C. Worship

    1. State here the commitment you are making to attend the worship services

of your choice during the next twelve months.

2. Again be as specific as you can, so also state the church or synagogue you will attend.

D. Stewardship

  1. State here the commitment you are making to a life of Stewardship. Explain how your life will be evident of our having an "Attitude of Gratitude" for all the gifts you have been so blessed with.

  2. Time

    a. State here how you will use your time you have been blessed with to practice stewardship in your life

  3. Talent

    a. State here how you use the talents you have been blessed with to practice stewardship in your life

  4. Treasures

    a. State here how you will use the treasures you have been blessed with to practice stewardship in your life

E. My Faith Community of Believers.

  1. State here the commitment you are making to your involvement in the Faith Community of your choice.

  2. State the degree of your involvement and how that involvement will attribute to the vitality of the life of the community.

Once you've completed the exercise, you must not file it away as if it were a time capsule. The first thing you should do is to share it with someone with whom you have a close relationship. The mere fact that you are willing to share your plan with someone to whom you can be accountable helps to cement in your own mind the commitment that you have toward your plan and the clarity you have in your vision. Sharing it with someone, especially someone who will share in that future life that you envision, will help bring your vision into reality.

The second thing you need to do is to post your plan where you can see it every day. I myself post mine on the wall in my closet. While it's not posted for the world to see, it's very visible for *me* to see each and every day of my life. Every day as I take my clothes from my closet, I am reminded of the plan I have implemented and the vision I have of the fruits of this plan. Every day I am reminded that with God's help, today will bring me one step closer to the goals I have set for my life, and thus, to the life that I desire.

The third thing you need to do is to realize that your *Life's Strategic Plan* must be a living document. It is printed on paper, not etched in stone. As you accomplish each short-term goal, cross it off as an acknowledgement of your success. There is a real therapeutic feeling you get from visibly seeing your progress toward the life you desire.

Second, you need to realize that there will be those times in life, and we will all have them sooner or later, when events will happen or circumstances will necessitate a change in either the primary long-term plans or in the short-term goals you have set to achieve the life you desire. These events or circumstances may be something good or not so good. If you were to win the state lottery of several millions, for example, chances are very good that may change some of your goals. Likewise, if you had a major financial setback or a serious illness or an accident, that may also change the timetable of some of your goals, if not even the actual goal itself. While events of life may change your goals, they do not have to change your primary mission statement. The changing of your goals due to unforeseen events or circumstances should not prohibit you from having the life you desire or from *being* the person you know God is calling you to be. All it means is that you have to attain that life through a different avenue or course.

You must be the master of your plan; you must never let your plan be the master of you. Realizing that this is a working and living document, you must also make it your commitment to revisit it annually, about the same time each year. For me, I personally like to use the week between Christmas and New Years as the traditional time to revisit my *Life's Strategic Plan*. Upon revisiting it, you will be able to make the adjustments necessary to account for those goals you have already accomplished, those which need to be adjusted due to unforeseen circumstances, adjustments due to your maturing in life and having your needs and desires change, and most importantly, the adding of any new goals you may now have.

The final thing you must do is to involve God as your Creator and Savior in every aspect of your plan. From the first breath you take in the morning till the last you take each night, you must keep Him as the "Objective" of your life. Without Him as your "Objective," your plan and your life will be meaningless—here today and gone tomorrow, like a house built on sand.

Conclusion

Congratulations. You have just taken control of your life. You have just set the course not only for the destination of where it is that you want your life to take you, but just as important, you have set out in complete detail the precise goals you will seek to accomplish in order to attain your desired life and become the person you desire to be. As I mentioned earlier, according to the United States Small Business Administration, less than 3% of Americans will ever accomplish the task of establishing goals and creating a vision of life such as you have just done. For that, again I say congratulations.

While congratulations are definitely in order, your real work has now only just begun. Anne Frank once said, "How wonderful it is that nobody need wait a single moment before starting to improve the world." In the same light, you need not wait another single moment before starting to improve *your* world. It all begins with you and the commitment you are making to the changes and improvements in the life that you desire. No one else can do it for you. No one else can motivate you, as your motivation must come from within, out of your desire and your ability to envision the life you want.

Vaclav Havel, former President of the Czech Republic, has said, "Vision alone is not enough; it must be combined with venture. It is not enough to stare up the steps; we must step up the stairs." Regardless of how much thought and time you may have given to your *Life's Strategic Plan,* if you do not put your plan into action by taking that first step up the stairs, your plan will be no more than empty words on paper—a fairy tale story at best.

Above all, remember always that success and happiness come as a result of your "being," not the results of your "doing." Your "doing" in life may sometimes change depending upon the events and circumstances that life can sometimes present to you. But who you are as a person, as a child of God, does not change. With a proper focus on the priorities you have established, and a firm conviction that God will always remain the "Objective" of your life, you will be able to live your life to its fullest.

In closing, I would like to leave you reflecting on the words of this prayer of St. Thomas More:

O Lord give us a mind that is humble, quiet
peaceable, patient and charitable, and a taste
of your Holy Spirit in all our
thoughts, words, and deeds.
O Lord, give us a lively faith,
a firm hope,
a fervent charity,
a love of you.
Take from us all lukewarmness in meditation
and dullness in prayer.
Give us fervor and delight in thinking of you,
your grace, and your tender compassion toward us.
Give us, good Lord the grace to work
for the things we pray for.
Amen.

Endnotes

1   Survey by the Gallup Organization conducted May 2–4 2004 and published in article dated May 25, 2004 by Albert Winseman, Religion and Social Trends Editor

2   Article of Gallup Organization published March 23, 2004 and written by Frank Newport, Editor in Chief.

3   Surveys conducted by the Gallup Organization. Both surveys cited in an article from the Gallup organization written by Joseph Carroll

4   Surveys conducted by the Gallup Organization. Both surveys cited in an article from the Gallup organization written by Joseph Carroll

5   *The Yellow Brick Road*; Author William J. Bausch. Published by Twenty-Third Publications, Mystic, Ct. 06355. Third printing 2002

6   Results taken from an article published August 29, 2002 by Frank Newport of the Gallup Organization

7   *Faithful Listening*; Author Joan Muller, Publisher Sheed & Ward, PO Box 317, Oxford, UK

8   Survey cited in an article by the Gallup Organization and written by Lydia Saad January 05, 2005

9   *Happiness Is an Inside Job*; Author John Powell. Publisher Thomas More, An RCL Company, 200 East Bethany Drive, Allan , Texas 75002–3804

10   *Happiness Is an Inside Job*; Author John Powell. Publisher Thomas More, An RCL Company, 200 East Bethany Drive, Allan , Texas 75002–3804

11   *The Yellow Brick Road*; Author William J. Bausch. Published by Twenty-Third Publications, Mystic, Ct. 06355. Third printing 2002

12   *Benedict's Way*; Authors Lonni Collins Pratt and Daniel Homan, O.S.B. Publisher Loyola Press, 3411 N. Ashland Avenue, Chicago, Illinois 60657

13   *Benedict's Way*; Authors Lonni Collins Pratt and Daniel Homan, O.S.B. Publisher Loyola Press, 3411 N. Ashland Avenue, Chicago, Illinois 60657

14   *The Life You've Always Wanted*; Author John Ortberg. Publisher Zondervan, Grand Rapids, Michigan 49530

15   Article published by the Gallup Organization dated November 04, 2003 by Heather Mason

16   Time Magazine published the April 24, 1989 article entitled *How America Has Run Out of Time* by Nancy Gibbs

17   Cited in an article from the Gallup Organization dated February 12, 2002 and written by David W. Moore, Senior Gallup Poll Editor

18   Dr. Eve Van Cauter, PhD, professor of medicine at the University of Chicago published in an article December 6, 2004 "*Sleep Loss Boosts Appetite, May Encourage Weight Gain*"

19   *Parenting isn't for Cowards* by Dr. James C. Dobson. World Books Publisher, Wayco, Texas

20   Coping with the 80's Author Joel Wells,
      Chicago: Thomas More Press, 1986

21   *Time Magazine*'s June 6th, 1983, cover
      story entitled *Stress: Can We Cope* by
      Claude Wallis

22   Cited from an article entitled "America's
      #1 Health Problem" by The American
      Institute of Stress, 124 Park Ave Yonkers
      New York, NY 10703)

23   Cited from the National Institute
      for Occupational Safety and Health
      Publication *#99–101*

24   Cited from Northwestern National Life
      Insurance Company, now ReliaStar
      Financial Corporation, (1991). Employee
      burnout: America's newest epidemic.
      Minneapolis, MN

25   1997 national study of the changing
      workforce conducted and published
      by the Family and Work Institute, New
      York, New York

26   Cited from an 2004 article published by
      the Stress, Anxiety, Depress Resource
      Center

27   *The Crises of Hope*; Author Edward
      Wojcicki. Publisher The Thomas More
      Press, 205 West Monroe Street Chicago,
      Ill

28   In December of 1995 Grady McAllister
      gave a presentation at the University of
      Houston College of Technology. In his
      presentation he cited a quote by Harvard
      Economics Professor, Juliet B. Schor

29   David Spiegel quote cited from an article
      entitled Stress-Busters: What Works by
      the Academic Skill Center, Dartmoth
      College 2001 in which the publisher of
      the article excerpted from an article by
      Geoffrey Cowley–Newsweek June 14,
      1999

30   National Mental Health Association
      quote cited as published in NMHA
      MHIC Fact sheet: Stress–Coping with
      Everyday Problems

31   National Mental Health Association
      quote cited as published in NMHA
      MHIC Fact sheet: Stress–Coping with
      Everyday Problems

32   Newsweek Magazine Article entitled
      "Talking to God: "An intimate look at the

way we pray." January 6, 1992)

33   *The Life You've Always Wanted*; John
     Ortberg. Zondervan, Grand Rapids,
     Michigan.

34   *International Standard Bible
     Encyclopedia* James Orr, M.A., D.D.,
     General Editor. Publisher Parsons
     Technology, Inc. Cedar Rapids, Iowa

35   Gallup Poll Published in a Commentary
     dated February 10, 2004 by Author
     Albert Winseman, Editor for Religious
     and Social Trends for the Gallup
     Organization.

To contact Dan Hoeger or to order
more copies of this book, contact

TATE PUBLISHING, LLC

127 East Trade Center Terrace
Mustang, Oklahoma 73064

(888) 361 - 9473

Tate Publishing, LLC

www.tatepublishing.com